THE E

THE EVANGELICALS

by

JOHN C. KING

HODDER AND STOUGHTON

Copyright © 1969 by John C. King
FIRST PRINTED 1969
SBN: 340 10772 3

All rights reserved. No part of this publication may be reproduced or transmitted in any form or by any means, electronic or mechanical, including photocopy, recording, or any information storage and retrieval system, without permission in writing from the publisher.

This book is sold subject to the condition that it shall not, by way of trade or otherwise, be lent, re-sold, hired out or otherwise circulated without the publisher's prior consent in any form of binding or cover other than that in which this is published and without a similar condition including this condition being imposed on the subsequent purchaser.

Printed in Great Britain for Hodder and Stoughton Limited, St. Paul's House, Warwick Lane, London, E.C.4, by Cox & Wyman Limited, London, Fakenham and Reading.

Contents

Foreword

To every group there comes a moment of clarity, a moment when issues are defined and choices become possible. Such a moment came to this generation of Evangelicals in the Church of England in 1967 when, from every corner of the kingdom, they made their way to Keele University in Staffordshire for the first National Evangelical Anglican Congress. The Congress was remarkable not so much for the lengthy statement it agreed as for the fact that it proved a focal point of many trends in Evangelicalism over the preceding ten or twenty years. During seven of those years it was my privilege to edit the *Church of England Newspaper*, to observe the trends and to encourage those that seemed to be the result of alert, biblical, realistic thinking. The Keele congress showed the trends for what they were. Keele took the lid off contemporary Evangelicalism; it let the cat out of the bag (and set it among the pigeons); it inspected the apology of a policy that had served the movement since 1928 and argued out an appropriate response to present needs. In short, Keele made plain the possibility of a renewal of Evangelicalism.

It is in the aftermath of Keele that Evangelicals in the Church of England must decide where their future lies. The choice as I understand it is between old habits (safe) and new ways (risky)—or, to put it another way, between conformity to an obsolete pattern and obedience to the Gospel. This view of the matter is of course a personal one; it may not be shared by any other Evangelical. However, on my departure from the editorial chair I thought it might possibly be useful to set down very rapidly my own assessment of Evangelicals today and my hopes for Evangelicals tomorrow. I believe that we Evangelicals *have* a future, but only if we are prepared for creative, risk-taking courses. Perhaps this personal assessment may have some slight share in nerving the N E A C constituency to make a right choice while choice is still possible.

CHAPTER ONE

People who know they are saved

In the Church of England today one group of churchmen gets less than its proper attention. Partly this is
because the members of the group represent an un-
fashionable point of view (and fashion is a not unim-
portant factor in ecclesiastical judgments, as elsewhere);
partly it is because they are not understood and consequently not liked; partly it is because they prefer, like
little Jack Horner, to get on with things in their own
corner without bothering the rest of the Church very
much. But quite as important as any of these factors is
the fact that these people claim to know that they are
saved; at least, this is the characteristic which chiefly
impresses others who have dealings with them.

The group in question is that comprising the
Evangelicals—and, since others also lay claim to this
title, the adjective "Conservative" has to be added to
the label. The need to add this adjective annoys
Evangelicals because in their view the word "Evangelical" is sufficient; but since in common parlance the
word "Evangelical" is insufficient in itself, the cumber-
some description is necessary in the same way as the

expression "Roman Catholic" is necessary (even though resented) to describe Christians submitting to the Roman obedience. From this point on, then, the word "Evangelical" will be generally used in what follows to signify those who describe themselves as, and are described by others as, Conservative Evangelicals. The full title will be used occasionally as a reminder that there are others who claim the unqualified title "Evangelical".

The question of assurance, of knowing that you are saved, deserves attention. It could indeed be regarded as the key to an understanding of the Evangelical position. For whether he is inside or outside the Church of England, the Evangelical believes that a man can not only *become* a Christian by putting his trust in Christ; he can *know* that he is a Christian and that his sins are forgiven. It is this certainty, this assurance, that marks out the Evangelical from his fellow-Christians.

Often the sense of assurance becomes uncomfortably apparent to others. The teacher who has just been supervising a lunch-hour Bible study at school and has now got to his cheese and biscuits is still mildly astonished by the views of those sixth-formers who know that they are saved and believe in a literal Adam and Eve. His colleague consoles him with the thought that such simple-minded black and white beliefs are at least refreshing—even if they are likely to be discarded lock, stock and barrel in the rough and tumble of university life.

Evangelical certainty varies not only in degree but in kind from one person to another. One person will give considerable weight to "the witness of the Spirit", an interior experience of the work of the Holy Spirit; another will almost entirely discount this aspect of the matter and will argue that assurance consists in nothing more or less than taking God at his word. On this point, as on others, Evangelicals are not in such close agreement as is sometimes thought.

The confidence of Evangelicals can be paralleled by the confidence of Roman Catholics. The comparison throws into relief the distinctive nature of Evangelical assurance. The Roman Catholic enjoys membership of a Church which has so clarified its doctrines and duties over the centuries that a member of it can be clear about his own standing and responsibilities at any given moment; there are no fluffy areas—everything is precise, orderly and comprehensible. A Roman Catholic can enjoy a sense of having done all that God can reasonably require. If all do their duty, the Church functions efficiently. The Roman Catholic layman goes about his duties in the knowledge that by doing his duty as the Church has interpreted it for him he is pleasing God. If he were asked whether he knew that he was a Christian, he would say that he had been baptised. If he were asked whether he had any better evidence than that, he would ask what better evidence there could be. The conception of some kind of inward assurance of personal salvation would be foreign to his understanding of Christianity.

If you asked an Evangelical how he knew he was a Christian, it is almost certain that you would not hear baptism mentioned. The Evangelical would tell you that there came a day when he put his trust in Christ, took Christ at his word and found a new sense of security as a result. Conversation would establish that his faith was a matter not of belonging to a Church, but of personal commitment to Christ. Christianity, he would say, is a matter not of fulfilling duties precisely laid down by ecclesiastical superiors, but of being rightly related to God through Christ. Baptism, he would say, does not save a man by making him a member of the Church; it is a sign which follows when a man has initially put his faith in Christ. The sacraments are not so much a divinely ordained apparatus by which men get into touch and remain in touch with God; they are rather signs confirming an already vigorous personal faith. The sense of assurance possessed to a greater or lesser degree by Evangelicals is not in fact an Evangelical invention; it merely takes a distinctive form and is given a particular emphasis by Evangelicals. That distinctive and emphatic form is not best understood by taking too seriously the egregious claims made by eager novices who are enjoying their first delightful taste of the Christian Gospel.

It is vigorous personal faith which is indispensable in Evangelical eyes, and it is for this reason that

Evangelicals often seem to be only faintly interested in Church order, Church unity, Church reorganisation and social issues. Their hearts are really in something else—the always urgent task of bringing men and women to the personal knowledge of Christ that has made all the difference in their own lives.

The magnitude of this difference between the Evangelical and his other Christian brothers should not be underestimated. The Evangelical may join in the same prayers, sing the same hymns and believe the same doctrines as do his fellow-Christians, but the emphasis which he gives to certain aspects of Christianity transforms his faith into something quite different. As far as he is concerned, the organisation, the repairing of inter-Church unity—even the sacraments themselves—are part of the framework of religion. The first thing is men's relationship with Christ; somehow men and women must be brought to see that without Christ they are lost. If they do not see this, all the religious framework in the world will do them no good. So whereas another member of the Church will go to great pains to repair or improve the "religious framework", because he believes that by doing this he is bringing Christ nearer to people, the Evangelical is more likely to be found going to great pains to deliver an evangelistic message designed to lead men to Christ, directly, urgently and—as likely as not—in a hall or other meeting-place where the "religious framework" is non-existent.

It is this insistence on personal commitment to Christ and the characteristic assurance of salvation that follows which is the differentiating mark of the Evangelical. In Evangelical eyes, to be a Christian is not merely to believe the articles of the Creed; there is an additional dimension to belief which can scarcely be put into words; it can only be shared. Those who are not Evangelicals find this difficult to understand; it almost seems that Evangelicals believe themselves to be the only true Christians.

A man does not of course have to belong to the Church of England to be a (Conservative) Evangelical. Contingents are found amongst the Baptists, the Congregationalists, the Methodists and other Free Churches. A capacity to make himself at home in varying ecclesiastical situations is one of the factors making for the survival of the Evangelical; this capacity for adaptation also suggests that the essence of Evangelicalism has little to do with principles of church government or historian continuity. It is probably true to say that most Evangelicals regard such matters as of secondary importance. What they regard as of primary importance is to be seen in the basis of their co-operation for practical purposes—e.g. a Billy Graham or an Eric Hutchings evangelistic campaign. In practical terms this includes the practice of preaching for a verdict, a clear and definite idea of what it means to be a Christian, and acceptance of the view that a man can be assured of his salvation.

Evangelicals in the Church of England are forgotten men. No matter how indignantly some bishops may claim to represent Evangelicals at the top level of the Church, it remains true that Evangelicals do not believe they have one spokesman of episcopal rank in this country. Despite their numbers Evangelicals have had to face the fact that their influence has been limited by lack of scholarship and a dearth of Evangelical heavyweights in positions of responsibility in the Church. Since bishops, in the popular view, are uniquely qualified spokesmen in the Church, Evangelicalism never gets a hearing; its case goes by default. People gain the impression that Evangelicals are little more than a noisy minority within the Church of England, that Evangelical opinions are indeed unacceptable (and possibly even infantile and subversive). Whether Evangelical opinions are infantile or subversive is a subject in its own right; it can scarcely be denied, however, that a false impression of an institution is gained when the opinions of a significant minority are ignored. Again, whether the absence of Evangelical bishops is put down to lack of men of appropriate calibre, to the reluctance of good men to become bishops, or to the readiness of Evangelicals to believe too much at a time when many in the Church are believing as little as possible, it must be acknowledged that the balance of power at the top level of the Church of England does not adequately reflect the disposition of forces lower down the scale. For whatever cause, Evangelicals in the

Church of England are given less attention than they ought to have.

The existence of Evangelicals is now being brought to the attention of those who manage to take seriously the considerable output of reports from official Church of England sources and the debates in Church Assembly. The Anglican-Methodist report, *The Scheme*, had, for example, a dissenting note by Dr J. I. Packer; the report on inter-communion had a statement by Gervase Duffield. Both Dr Packer and Mr Duffield are well-known Evangelicals. In Church Assembly the presence of Evangelicals is not unnoticed; a notable instance of Evangelical influence was the refusal by the House of Laity to approve the form of Confirmation service used by most bishops; as a consequence the bishops were obliged promptly to restrict themselves to the 1662 form for a period.

However, the number of people who read all the Church of England reports and take a close interest in Church Assembly debates is severely limited. The reputation enjoyed by Evangelicals therefore rests upon vague associations with Billy Graham and an equally vague reputation for controversy and obstructionism. Not realising that the conduct of Church of England business depends to a large extent on who draws up the agenda, the casual onlooker regards opponents of official business as trouble-makers impeding the work of men of goodwill.

The tendency to associate Evangelicals with Billy

Graham is not altogether illuminating. It is far from true to say that Evangelicals today are starry-eyed about Billy Graham and his evangelistic methods, and it is equally far from the truth to suggest that most Evangelicals have only a rudimentary theology which starts with the act of creation in 4004 B C and ends with unbelievers being consigned to everlasting punishment.

Those who are personally acquainted with Evangelicals know that the reputation for bigotry and negative participation is not altogether deserved. Like others, many Evangelicals are not convinced that the Church of England is heading entirely in the right direction at the present time; if they give voice to their hesitations and propose other policies, they are doing what many vigorous churchmen are doing at the present time.

As the Jew is to be found throughout the nations of the world—at home, acclimatised and yet separate from his fellow-countrymen—so the Conservative Evangelical is to be found throughout the Churches of the world, an Anglican among the Anglicans, a Baptist among the Baptists, a Congregationalist among the Congregationalists, yet distinguished from his fellows by a supra-Church loyalty that makes him in some ways more like his fellow-Evangelicals than like his fellow-churchmen. The Evangelical himself would say that his first loyalty was to Christ and his Word; imperfectly explained, this attitude might be interpreted

B

as stand-offish and reserved. It might provoke misunderstanding and reserve in turn. That Evangelicals in the Church of England have been misunderstood is sufficient reason for looking at them in some detail.

CHAPTER TWO

But how do you recognise them?

Evangelicals in the Church of England are not numerous. Perhaps one clergyman in eight is an Evangelical. It is therefore perfectly possible for good Church of England people to go to church for a life-time without meeting one. It may be understood that Mr X down the road at Christ Church is "very low", and therefore, somehow, not very nice; but as for understanding Mr X's particular emphasis in present-ing Christianity or inquiring what makes him the "low" churchman he is, there just is not time. The autumn sale or the garden party or the patronal festival or some other part of the Christian framework needs attention. Mr X remains the oddity down the road.

But many may have met an Evangelical without realising it. Odd though they may be, Evangelicals do not normally ride tradesmen's bicycles decorated with Scripture texts; nor do they usually pester strangers with questions about the salvation of their souls (though I have known of Evangelicals who *have* done these things). Nowadays Evangelicals arc likely to be person-able young clergymen with a natural good humour and a fair ration of charm. They have private enthusiasms for riding, sailing, antiques or some other interest. Not many go as far as breeding horses (though I know one who does), but all in all the Evangelical today is a warm-hearted human being who enjoys his leisure-time as much as the next man.

An Evangelical vicar today is likely to be a young man with a taste for electronics who is rather amused by the idea of living in a rambling mansion, and has turned his decaying butler's pantry into a photographic darkroom. His young family takes up a good deal of his time and he has (perhaps regretfully) little time for dusty theological tomes. He believes in Christ's Gospel enthusiastically and he wants his parishioners to enjoy what he enjoys himself. When he meets another dedicated Christian person, he is not so much concerned about the particular denominational label he wears as about his living faith in Christ.

Such a man probably has a grotesquely unsuitable Victorian church with a roof fund attached. He goes along with diocesan regulations about faculties and wryly pays for the privilege of obtaining permission to spend money on a building whose utility is questionable. He is less inclined to go along with regulations which have the effect of denying to non-Anglicans an entrance to the Communion Table in the church of which he is vicar. In his view any believer in Christ should be welcome as a visitor—and this is made plain in his notices in church on Sunday.

This young enthusiast cheerfully does his duty in his parish; he also keeps in touch with others of like mind, even though keeping in touch may mean occasional journeys of two or three hours across a couple of counties. He believes that he has something worthwhile and distinctive to preserve, and he finds the companionship of other Evangelicals a reinforcement to his convictions which is not to be found in the typical chapter meeting for neighbouring clergymen of all outlooks.

In the parish of St Paul, Elswick, Newcastle-upon-Tyne, for example, half a dozen nationalities are cheek-by-jowl. The parish church is a big, grime-laden Gothic structure equally unsuited for the handful of saints or the multitude of the indifferent for whose benefit it is putatively intended. Manning this ill-equipped Anglican strongpoint, Peter Cook, a young family man, has the task of demonstrating the meaning and power of the Gospel in an area of shattered houses, slums and squalor. The traditional language of Anglican worship is as far removed from Elswick speech as the language of Chaucer is removed from that of most of us; there are no polished suburban leaders. St Paul's could be held to symbolise the bankruptcy of the traditional parochial system; it also represents the increasing number of down-town churches where Evangelical Christianity is losing some of its social accretions and finding its own soul.

It is now possible to find, as once it was not, young Evangelical clergymen serving as industrial chaplains,

specialising in work amongst drug-addicts and exploit-
ing the opportunities in city centres. Nobody takes on
forms of ministry like these without being willing to
learn, and this again is something far removed from the
distasteful reputation gained in the past by Evangelicals
who gave the impression of knowing all the answers and
therefore being under no necessity to explore, experiment or inquire.

Tell-tale characteristics that show a clergyman to be
an Evangelical are: his dress (normally he wears a
surplice and scarf at all services and does *not* wear a
stole; out and about the parish he does *not* favour a
cassock); his habit of standing sideways for Holy Communion (the north side position as opposed to the east-
ward position, which involves turning your back on the
congregation); his distaste for candles, frontals, turning
east for the Creed, bowing to the Communion Table,
and very young Confirmation candidates. He rates
prayer meetings highly and sees nothing unusual in
Christian people opening their mouths in prayer in the
presence of other Christians. He is a keen supporter of
missionaries and is enthusiastic about the church bookstall.

An Evangelical is soon identified by his vocabulary.
He employs characteristic phrases. He will not talk of
being "laid aside on a bed of sickness" unless he is a
very old-fashioned Evangelical indeed, but he may well
refer to "believers" where other Anglicans would refer
to "the faithful". He will refer to himself as a minister

rather than a priest (although priest is of course a prayer book term) and will discourage people from calling him "Father". He will not have many occasions to refer to "confessors" or "spiritual directors" and he will not announce confessions on Saturday evening. "Holy Communion" and "Lord's Supper" are his preferred terms for the sacrament of Christ's body and blood; he may or may not favour the expression "Eucharist" (although this is of course derived from a word used in the New Testament). "Morning Prayer" and "Evening Prayer" are preferred expressions; "Mattins" and "Evensong", though found in the prayer book, are avoided by Evangelicals. It must be added that with the supersession of the 1662 prayer book proceeding apace, these phraseological differences are becoming old hat, and many Evangelicals are aware of this.

An Evangelical does not like raffles, whist drives, bingo, dances in the parish hall or any form of alcohol. He does like prayer meetings, Bible classes, hymn-singing and direct giving. (He was practising and preaching what is now described as stewardship long before it enjoyed its present vogue.) His sermons are long (often too long, as his people will readily protest) and he favours extempore prayer. He is more concerned to get people converted than to get them confirmed.

The number of Evangelical clergymen must not of course be taken as a guide to the overall number of Evangelicals in the country at large. An Evangelical parish must be regarded as nothing more definite than a parish with an Evangelical clergyman. Strong as the vicar's views may be, it is probable that few in the parish share them—or even know what they are all about. An Evangelical clergyman may be appointed by a private patron who is not in the least interested in clerical niceties but takes a fancy to a likeable young man who is patently sincere. I can think of more than one clergyman who is now happily doing his job in a parish that had probably never heard the word "Evangelical" before he was appointed. What such parishes find important—and indeed they may refer to this in their resolution about a new vicar—is that they shall not have their candlesticks or bell-ringers or frontals disturbed. Such naïvety smoothes the path of the incoming incumbent, who knows he is free to put his own doctrinal impress on the parish provided the candlesticks are not disturbed, but it can make for a credibility gap as the vicar pushes on with a programme that has only the uncomprehending support of parishioners quite unaware of what their vicar is aiming at. It is in such parishes that laymen are particularly likely to meet an Evangelical without knowing it.

An Evangelical parish, then, must be distinguished from an Evangelical incumbent. In the course of years the incumbent may be expected to grow his own crop of young Evangelicals, but this process is likely to happen only in the flourishing suburban belt where Evangelical religion "takes".

Not all Evangelicals are clergymen, of course, but in

general the distinctive flavour of Evangelicalism is found most noticeably in the full-time professional, the man who has had time to develop opinions on doctrinal matters. There *are* Evangelical laymen, and some of them are energetically engaged in the House of Laity of Church Assembly, but Evangelical laymen tend to be either inter-denominational and independent (preaching for example in Non-conformist churches as much as in Church of England churches), or more Anglican than the clergy themselves. Lay initiative is a delicate plant in the Church of England at all levels—and the plant does not flourish noticeably better in Evangelical parishes than elsewhere.

Female Evangelicals exist, but it is doubtful if Evangelicalism would survive if its survival depended entirely upon its woman-power. For if lay initiative is a delicate plant in the Church of England, the idea of giving responsibility to women is a more delicate growth still, and a good many Evangelicals are as suspicious as any other group in the Church about women's ministry. The influence of the Brethren (formerly the Plymouth Brethren) probably accounts for this outlook.

However, clergy-dominated though they may be, Evangelical lay people are to be found where the action is. In the summer Evangelicals are to be found helping in seaside missions (run by the Scripture Union), holiday camps (run by the Church Pastoral-Aid Society, Pathfinders, Campaigners, etc) and parish missions (organised by the Inter-Varsity Fellowship).

Evangelical lay people say grace at meals, conduct family prayers, attend prayer meetings and back up visiting campaigns and other evangelistic efforts.

Other examples of this self-forgetful readiness to share the good things of Christ with others are not hard to find. Amongst young people in particular Evangelical vitality has an agreeable freshness. All over the country teenage Pathfinders attend weekly meetings of their Bible class groups and go to rallies, house-parties and camps. The big brother of Pathfinders, the Church Youth Fellowships Association, has filled St Paul's Cathedral. Movements like these have their own ways of showing their authenticity; new Christian songs like those found in *Youth Praise* and a readiness to explore drama in worship (as at the C Y F A rally in St Paul's) indicate that when it gets into its stride Evangelicalism can show a creativity which others might envy.

Self-forgetful readiness to serve is seen abundantly today in down-town parishes where Evangelicalism is no fugitive and cloistered virtue. Probably by now most of the parish of St Jerome and St Silas, Ardwick, Manchester, has been demolished, but as this section of Manchester fell before the bulldozers, pockets of resistance were kept going until the end. A Sunday school met in a doomed building as the demolishers drew near, and continued to meet as long as there were children in the neighbourhood. This kind of cheerful willingness to back a loser for the sake of the Gospel is a very different thing from calculated efforts to pester people into an unvarying conversion experience—and it is this which has gained Evangelicals a bad name in many quarters.

It must be acknowledged that Evangelicalism is a clergy-dominated male movement in the Church. Much though its supporters would like it to be regarded as a unique repository of the genuine New Testament emphasis in religion (and sometimes even a latter-day equivalent of the Old Testament remnant), honesty compels one to admit that, strong as it is in many departments, its follies and shortcomings are plain for all to see; only its coyness has prevented the public gaze from being directed too searchingly at those follies and shortcomings hitherto.

CHAPTER THREE

Performance figures

In some fields Evangelicals are putting up as robust a performance as any group in the Church of England. Missionary support is one such field. A few facts and figures at random will illustrate this. In the summer of 1968 Emmanuel church, Northwood, Middlesex, held its annual gift day. The target was £3,000, of which half, it was announced, would help to pay off outstanding sums on the new organ and half would go to missionary causes. At the end of the gift day (which was preceded by a night of prayer) the result was announced: £3,464.

It is not only for missionary purposes that efforts are made. Men of the Saviour church, Blackburn, Lancs, organised a sixteen-mile sponsored walk in aid of the church's dry rot and organ fund. Over 200 church members took part in the walk; it raised £780. In the summer of 1968 twenty young people belonging to St Luke's church, Watford, Herts, clocked a total of 2,500 sponsored miles' cycling and raised £465 for a new church hall.

At Christ Church, Bromley, Kent, the annual gift

day in the autumn of 1967 brought in £3,356—£2,906 for a new hall project and £450 for missionary causes.

At Christmas, 1967, St Mary of Bethany church, Woking, Surrey, set out to raise sufficient money (£325) to enable "Shelter" to house one family. This effort was to be in addition to existing missionary giving. Among the gifts which came in was one for £325. St Mary's promptly raised its sights and asked for another £325; the necessary money was forthcoming.

Not all Evangelical churches believe in gift days. Some prefer the systematic form of giving known as stewardship. In the autumn of 1967 Christ Church, Downend, Bristol, held a thanksgiving week to celebrate seven years "without gift days or other fund-raising activities". During the seven years £32,000 had been received in pledged giving.

One expects Evangelicals to support Billy Graham crusade meetings. The relays organised in connection with the "All Britain Crusade" held in 1967 were strongly supported by Evangelicals in the Church of England. St George's church, Huyton, Liverpool, ran a seventy-two-seater bus eight miles to the Empire theatre every night except Sunday during the period of the relays. An average of fifty people made use of the service each night.

One Sunday in June, 1968, students from York University picketed ten so-called redundant churches, protesting against the wealth of the Church at a time of world poverty. They handed out leaflets to those attending services. One of the churches to be picketed was St Cuthbert's. When the picket entered the church, he found that not one seat out of the 200 seats available was empty. The Rev David Watson, an Evangelical, who was ministering in the church, said that the church had at one time been included on the redundant list, and that it was this which had led the students to include it in their schedule.

When new vestries, offices, a kitchen and accommodation for the Rector of St Helen's, Bishopsgate, in the City of London, were dedicated in January, 1968, it was reported that nearly 100 lunches were being served each Tuesday to people attending the lunch-hour services. About 500 city workers, it was said, were regularly present at these services, led by the Rector, the Rev Dick Lucas.

Children's holiday clubs are another field in which Evangelicals are active. A "Good News Week" run in conjunction with the Methodists at Bramcote, Notts, in the spring of 1968 was attracting 300 children a day by the time it ended; teenagers packed a "7.30 Special" meeting each evening.

Evangelicals are well-known for their enthusiasm for youth work. Broads cruises, trips abroad, camps and house-parties are honoured features of the Evangelical programme arranged for young people each summer. Not so predictable was the passion play written by the young people (Platters, as they call themselves) of Holy Trinity, Platt, Manchester. Twenty-six young people wrote the play at the suggestion of their Rector, the Rev Michael Baughen, and with the guidance of their curate, the Rev Robert Warren. It scarcely needs saying that the play packed the hall when it was performed at Easter, 1968.

A moonlight barbecue organised by the young people's fellowship of Christ Church, Virginia Water, Surrey, in the summer of 1968 was advertised by psychedelic posters and attended by between four and five hundred teenagers. Revolving coloured spot-lights picked out two Christian pop groups as they sang in a clearing in the woods.

New approaches to publicity and print are not un-common. When Christ Church, Richmond, Surrey, organised a "Family of God" week-end in November, 1967, 25,000 paper bags carrying the slogan "Hear Neville Knox" were used to advertise the event. News-paper-format publications issued at irregular intervals through the year (as at St Peter's, Harold Wood, Essex) are also examples of good letter-box material.

Evangelicals have taken a leading part in the drive to make church bookstalls an accepted feature of church life and to ensure that they bear comparison with book displays elsewhere. In its 1968 annual church bookstall survey the *Church of England Newspaper* listed five churches, all Evangelical, with bookstalls having a turn-over of £500 or more. The survey included details of 105 bookstalls, mostly in Evangelical churches, with a turnover of £20,980 in that year. The *C E N* is an

Evangelical weekly, so one would expect its bookstall survey to be well served with information from that section of the Church, but there is little doubt that bookstalls are a particularly strong feature in Evangelical parishes.

CHAPTER FOUR

Why do they stand apart?

The Conservative Evangelical is a man who knows that Christ has forgiven his sins. This sense of assurance is the flower of a theological plant that roots in a self-interpreting authoritative Bible and has as its main stem the basic Christian doctrines of the Trinity leading into the doctrine of the saving work of Christ on the cross; the Evangelical interprets that work as having its application to the sinner purely through faith. The distinctive characteristic is, in theological language, the doctrine of justification by faith alone.

To say this does not of course mean that a man must save himself by his own exertions. What it does mean is that God's grace has made possible a way for sinful men to escape judgment—and that way is through the sacrifice of Christ. To go that way a man has to receive forgiveness of sins as a free gift directly from God. He does not have to take part in a euchar-istic service (although the Evangelical agrees that this is an appropriate way for the converted man to say "thank you" to God and to be renewed in Christ); nor does he need the offices of another man (a priest) to

C

enable him to enter into a direct relationship with God through Christ.

The essence of the matter is that the man who turns to Christ for salvation gains a new standing, and he gains that new standing immediately, fully and irrevocably. No Christian can be more "justified" than any other Christian; and no Christian can go on to be more "justified" than he was when he first turned to Christ. "Justification" is an absolute term. It refers to standing, not character. A man can become more "sanctified" — but that is another story.

This is the doctrinal emphasis for which Luther stood and which Calvin made so distinctive a part of his theological system. The Conservative Evangelical, then, holds a Calvinist view of the Christian Gospel and believes that this interpretation is more truly biblical than any other. This interpretation, he would assert, is the interpretation advanced by the apostles and is also consistent with, and does justice to, the entire sweep of biblical revelation. (Needless to say, the Evangelical believes that Christianity is a revealed religion, not a system of belief or ritual laboriously compiled by the human mind.)

The Conservative Evangelical might add that his interpretation is one that has the backing of the Thirty-nine Articles; the Church of England, he would say, stands squarely in the Reformed tradition. It would, of course, be difficult for anyone to contest this. The Evangelical, then, is happy to stand, and to belong to a

Church which stands (so far as the question of man's salvation is concerned), in the Augustinian-Calvinist tradition.

If you believe that the Augustinian-Calvinist stream of doctrine is the legitimate successor to the apostles and their interpretation of the Gospel, then clearly Evangelicals have a high office to perform. They must do no less than call the Church to be true to itself. They must remind the Church that the biblical Gospel is a certain shape and that only a disservice is performed by distorting that shape. Holding such views of his responsibility, an Evangelical is likely to appear stand-offish to his non-Evangelical fellow-members of the Church of England.

The doctrinal emphasis of (Conservative) Evangelicalism is half the story. But it is only half, for this kind of doctrine is more or less shared by other Christians standing in the Reformed tradition. There is another characteristic and it is this which, as we have already suggested, gives Evangelicals as distinctive a character as Moral Re-Armers or spelling reformers. This determining characteristic is some kind of conversion-experience and a claim, implicit or explicit, to have had a personal experience of meeting Christ. Evangelicalism is about nothing if it is not about conversion and a direct encounter with the living Christ. When you see a group of Evangelicals together you realise that this experience is something they share with one another. It is also something which marks them off from those who have not had a similar experience. It must be added that there are differences of emphasis among Evangelicals; some would stress the personal, daily encounter with Christ more than the assurance resulting from being justified. In general, however, the shared experience is decisive.

It is this shared experience which enables Evangelicals to do what many other Christians would run a mile to avoid: give a testimony. This means speaking of one's personal faith and describing how one came to possess it. Evangelicals can cope with what to others is an intolerably exacting and embarrassing business because, to an Evangelical, becoming a Christian is coming to know Jesus, and so sure is his consciousness of Christ that he does not find it difficult to explain. (Some Evangelicals of course find it too easy to explain and once on their feet are unstoppable; others tend to copy one another's phrases so that one suspects the authenticity of their experience. But the discouragements to giving a testimony are so great that one must give credit where it is due and acknowledge that normally a man will not bare his soul in public unless he has counted the cost and has something to say.)

Evangelicals do not always succeed in maintaining a sense of proportion and a sense of humour (whereas Christ, it seems from the Gospels, maintained both) about the deep things of the spirit. As a consequence, Evangelicals sometimes give the unhappy impression of having a direct line to God which is not open to other mortals. For this there is no excuse; the only antidote is gentle mockery. But the fault springs from excessive zeal; Evangelicals are so concerned to preserve the truth of the Gospel as they understand it that they tend to lose a sense of proportion. At their best, however, Evangelicals are warm-hearted disciples of Christ, true to their convictions and wide in their sympathies.

It remains true, nevertheless, that what is regarded by Evangelicals as loyalty to essential truth is regarded by others as defensive and suspicious stubbornness. No human being will ever find it easy to combine humility with a deep conviction of the rightness of his cause, and Evangelicals are not above other men in this respect. Sometimes fear and personal inadequacy make for unnecessary barriers keeping away other Christians and depriving the Evangelical of new horizons he could well explore without abandoning his distinctive convictions. Sometimes the Evangelical forgets that there is always a two-way traffic in the meeting of minds, that he himself may influence the other person by putting a point charitably and with good humour.

Sometimes, too, Evangelicals forget the great issues that engaged the attention of their forefathers and differentiate themselves by over-scrupulous attention to shibboleths and passwords. Instead of wrestling with the problem of an oath of loyalty to an upstart monarch or the beginnings of a crusade against slavery, they give their attention to the question of where they should stand when they take the Communion service, whether they should light the candles and whether they should call themselves "parish priests". Compared with the great questions of spiritual and political liberty, these trivial matters get far more attention than they deserve from Evangelicals.

Many are the churchmen who would say, "Evangelicals have a great contribution to make to the Church as a whole." Such churchmen speak approvingly (and not without a hint of condescension towards, as it were, a junior partner) of the eagerness with which Evangelicals work amongst young people. And when Evangelicals show some sign of interest in the ecumenical movement they are full of hope for the future, for this is an indication that Evangelicals may one day recognise themselves as contributors to the coming great Church, instead of persisting in their tiresome, self-chosen role of monopolists of the truth.

Much as they would like to regard themselves as helpful contributors to a scheme of things drawn up by better and wiser men than themselves, Evangelicals cannot accept this pattern. Their theology compels them to say that certain beliefs are right and certain beliefs are wrong, and that no good purpose is served by aiming to produce a synthesis. When an Evangelical insists that the doctrine of justification by faith alone is a cardinal point of faith, he is not putting forward a contribution; he is isolating a determining factor. He is asking for a decision about where the Church stands on what Luther called the doctrine of a standing or a fall-

ing Church. On such points, he maintains, there can be
no compromise. The issue can scarcely be evaded by
saying that the matter is old-fashioned, that the debate
has moved on, that we no longer think in those terms.
The important question is: is this doctrine true? If it
is, then other matters must be brought into line, and if
necessary an overhauling of the doctrinal standards of
the Church must take place. It is because they have
insisted that this issue is of importance that Evangelicals
have stood apart and continue to prefer to do evangelistic work (to quote one specific example) with other
Evangelicals rather than with Anglicans in general.

CHAPTER FIVE

Not what they used to be

Evangelicals are not what they used to be. Thirty years ago they were, whatever their limitations, a recognisable party in the Church of England, a party of protest, a party united in opposition to attempts by Tractarians and fellow-travellers to change the face of the Established Church—and united more particularly to oppose the wickedness which had brought the 1928 prayer book into general use, with the connivance of the bishops. More and more, as a result, Evangelicals came to regard Parliament as an appropriate and God-given arbiter in matters ecclesiastical.

In those days Evangelicals were great supporters of the *status quo*. The Church of England by law established was seen as the fairest expression on God's earth of biblical Christianity; to touch its prayer book (in archaic language), its canons (dusty dead letters), or most of all its Articles was, in the eyes of Evangelicals, to touch the ark of the covenant. Evangelicals in other Churches might wonder at an Evangelicalism which so readily practised universal infant baptism and allowed the State to dictate its forms of worship; but criticism was mostly brushed aside with a confidence that was based on what were held to be impeccable doctrinal statements and a prayer book that, old-fashioned as it might be, was held to be a glorious form of worship packed with Scripture which deserved to be the cynosure of all Christian eyes. In short, pre-war Evangelicalism was secure, complacent, convinced of its own rectitude and stirred to fury only by misguided attempts, as they were believed to be, to tinker with a Church that was custom-built (well, almost) for Evangelicals.

Much has changed since those days. Everybody in the Church of England has now woken up to the fact that the 1662 Book of Common Prayer, noble as it is, is as ill-suited to congregational worship today as a seventeenth-century sewerage system is ill-suited to the needs of a new town. Nobody in the Church of England is entirely happy about the State deciding on forms of worship and the appointment of bishops. All agree that the question today is not so much what type of Church is most suitable for the Christian Englishmen (i.e. Englishmen baptised in infancy) as how to show Christianity to be meaningful to the man of leisure who has replaced the dutiful yokel.

Evangelicals, like others, are men of their age. The pre-war Evangelical only too easily identified himself and his cause with the decent middle-class defended by Baldwin, Chamberlain, the British Fleet and the White Cliffs of Dover. The Evangelical today finds this record

an embarrassing legacy and is less ready than a former
generation to defend ecclesiastical and other privilege
which sorts ill with an unprejudiced reading of the New
Testament.

Compared with their pre-war predecessors, Evangelicals today are flexible, teachable and open-minded. If
they are disorganised, it is because they prefer muddle
to membership of a party based on nothing better than
opposition to attempts to alter the *status quo*. If they
are less dogmatic than their fathers, it is because they
have repudiated the more woodwormy planks in their
fathers' Erastian platform. If they are more numerous
(as they undoubtedly are) without being any more in-
fluential in the Church at large, it is because they
resemble their fathers in being more concerned with
"preaching the Gospel" than in shaping the changing
Church.

Evangelicals did not of course come into being in
1928. The prayer book crisis merely drove them (or
some of them) together and had the effect of making
them take up fixed positions within which they indoc-
trinated succeeding generations. They feared that they
were being submerged by the triumphant Tractarians;
they suspected every new move in the Church to be
"the thin end of the wedge" (so that when canon law
revision came along, any dubious aspects in its history
were flourished abroad malevolently); they withdrew
more and more into their shell and consoled themselves
with the reflection that they were the true sons of the

Church of England, whilst others were interlopers grazing in foreign pastures.

Outclassed, cornered and despised, they might have had no connection at all with their forebears who had eagerly filled the Exeter Hall for evangelistic meetings, established one missionary society after another, sung the hymns of John Newton and William Cowper and been encouraged by the confident declarations of Bishop Ryle.

Evangelicalism arose in the train of the Methodist movement; it also claims other antecedents and these help to determine its character. The Reformers are regarded as progenitors of the Evangelicals because they settled the form of the Church of England, although they could hardly be regarded as Evangelicals, even in a proleptic sense. Nobody, for example, would describe Cranmer as an Evangelical. The Puritans are also regarded as occupying a prominent place in the family tree, although nobody would describe John Owen, for example, as an Evangelical.

It will not escape notice that Evangelicalism is something of an ecclesiastical mongrel. Its claim to be the true inheritor of the apostolic message may therefore be open to query; classical Puritans and Reformers may well be considered as having better credentials on the terms proposed by Evangelicals themselves.

The fact is that different Evangelicals trace their descent from different sources. One man looks back to the Puritans and preaches the way they did—

determinedly exhaustive sermons with plenty of hard intellectual content and a complete disregard for style. Another man looks back to Fletcher of Madeley and presses the need for personal conversion regardless, almost, of the constitution of the Church. Another man looks back to the Reformers or to Charles Simeon while yet another looks back hardly any further than the early days of the Keswick Convention. With all these strands making up the present-day Evangelical, it is not surprising that Evangelicals do not find it easy to stick together.

Neither is it surprising that Evangelicals should show changes, sometimes substantial, from one generation to another. Taboos have varied. John Newton, for instance, used to smoke, whereas it is uncommon today to find an Evangelical who does so. Similar differences are found in attitudes to alcohol. Strange to say, owners of cigarette factories and breweries have been outstanding benefactors of the Evangelical cause. Until recently it was possible to saddle Evangelicals with a uniform reputation for being philistine, provincial and platitudinous; it is now possible to detect the beginnings of a break-up in that particular log-jam.

It should not be overlooked that the interests of Evangelicals have changed over the years. Once they were preoccupied with revival; now little is heard about this, although there are still groups which meet regularly to devote a night or half a night to praying for revival. A creative approach to liturgy is now more likely to be in evidence than study of the overcoming life. The pre-war interest in adventism has almost disappeared; enthusiasm for coffee-bars and pop music could never have been predicted thirty years ago, but it is now a characteristic mark of upsurging Evangelicalism.

Perhaps the most important difference between Evangelicals today and Evangelicals of thirty years ago is that Evangelicals today are more numerous. In his epilogue to *The Church of England 1900–1965* (S C M Press) Roger Lloyd spoke of "the surprising but strong revival of biblical fundamentalism". Dismaying as he thought this to be, Roger Lloyd recognised that Conservative Evangelical Christian Unions were producing many ordination candidates and missionary volunteers. Instead of being a beleaguered dispirited minority, Evangelicals are now a vigorous group of men not content to skulk in their tents but ready to go abroad looking for fresh opportunities wherever they may be found in the Church of England. The difference in tone is quite unmistakable.

It is because Evangelicals are a growing force in the land that the Church as a whole needs to notice them. It is because Evangelicals scarcely know themselves that they need to look in a mirror. Things are not always what they seem to be; and the person who looks closely at Church of England Evangelicals today is likely to find himself looking at an altogether new phenomenon, alive, eager, confused and unco-ordinated. He may in fact be not unlike a man looking at the new style of poetry introduced to this country by Wyatt and Surrey. Round the corner, though he could not know it, were Spenser, Donne and Shakespeare.

CHAPTER SIX

True blue and otherwise

An Evangelical is a person who is assured that his sins are forgiven because he has put his trust in Christ. A difficulty arises. What about those people who have put their trust in Christ but do not have Calvinist convictions? Such people do exist; they are found in Lee Abbey circles, on the bench of bishops and in parishes which are full of (well, contain a sprinkling of) converted people yet are not on the C P–A S or Islington wavelength. Amongst the clergy such men are near the border between Conservative Evangelicals and Liberal Evangelicals; included in the borderline group are ex-Ridley Hall tutors, evangelistically-minded bishops and missionary experts. Also in the group are bishops who were once shining lights in Conservative Evangelical circles and clergymen, sometimes ordained in later life, who have had an authentic Evangelical experience but have somehow missed the usual process which stamps a man as clearly as though he has been through Eton, Christ Church and the Brigade of Guards. This Evangelical penumbra gives the true blue the fidgets; it confuses the clear distinction between Evangelical sheep and almost Evangelical goats.

Evangelicalism is seen in its pride at the Islington Clerical Conference. Held once a year in Church House, Westminster, this conference brings together a representative clutch of clergymen—college cronies re-united after the passage of years, country incumbents glad to have a day with fellow-clergymen of a similar outlook, more or less celebrated Keswick speakers, young vicars with mini-parishes, and the few surviving clerics who remember the days when Upper Street, Islington, was a rallying-point for Protestant Anglicans who saw the Church of England slipping away from its honoured formularies.

"Islington" is clearly true blue; so is the Church Pastoral-Aid Society. But beyond this opinions will differ. Simeon's Trustees will probably be recognised as acceptable; so will Church Society. (Indeed there are those who will leap to point out that Church Society is the citadel of Anglican Evangelical orthodoxy.) Among the missionary societies the Bible Churchmen's Mis-sionary Society and the South American Missionary Society will be unquestioned. But the Church's Min-istry among the Jews? And Lee Abbey? An entire spectrum is involved—a spectrum ranging from the Protestant Truth Society and the Fellowship of Evangelical Churchmen at one end of the scale to Ridley Hall and Lee Abbey at the other end. Clergy-men are placed on the spectrum—absurd though this may seem to the layman—according to their dress: whether they invariably wear a scarf and hood, or whether they are prepared to wear stoles or even the entire eucharistic vestments.

The spectrum is seen most clearly in that sensitive area, the theological colleges. Only four of the twenty-five or so theological colleges in the Church of England are unquestionably Evangelical—Tyndale Hall, Clifton, Oak Hill and the London College of Divinity. Cranmer Hall, Durham, is qualifying for a place in the sun. Ridley almost qualifies; Wycliffe and St Aidan's qualify less, and other colleges merely have individual Evangelical ordinands. The colleges are plainly key units in the Evangelical structure; they preserve the true blue tradition by ensuring a supply of Evangelical clergymen.

Basically, as has been said, the doctrinal requirement of the Evangelical movement is a Calvinist interpretation of the Gospel—which is why Evangelicals are so happy with the Thirty-nine Articles. Justification by faith alone is the key doctrine, and the sovereignty of Scripture is the determining factor in controversy.

There is, however, some degree of latitude in basic doctrine. The Church of England Evangelical Council, for example, regards the Bible as "supreme in its authority". The B C M S is more precise; point three of its basis begins: "Belief that the Canonical Books of the Old and New Testament are wholly trustworthy, historically as well as in matters of faith and

D

doctrine . . ." Some Evangelicals would regard it as essential to believe that Eve was created by sub-division from Adam and that the Garden of Eden could be geographically identified if a sufficient search were mounted. Other Evangelicals would be happy to accept the word "myth" about the Adam and Eve story.

Very few Evangelicals would in fact accept a thoroughgoing Calvinist interpretation of the Gospel. Calvin believed, for example, that Christ suffered the pains of hell (i.e. the tortures of a condemned and ruined man) when he descended there, but very few Evangelicals would be found to believe that today. The word "infallibility" would have to be very carefully considered before many Evangelicals could sign the doctrinal basis of the Inter-Varsity Fellowship. To accept that the Bible is infallible and to accept also that St Mark, for instance, is not very precise in his reporting (as R. A. Cole happily does in his Tyndale commentary on Mark) shows that the word "infallibility" does not mean what it appears to mean to the innocent inquirer.

The basic position of the Evangelicals comes up for consideration afresh as various elements in the Church of England formula attract attention. While churchmen could still point to the Thirty-nine Articles and the 1662 Book of Common Prayer as their title-deeds, loyalty to the Church of England was uncomplicated; the true complexity of the situation was concealed. But when the experimental services measure finally gained approval and the Church of England could legitimately begin a course of modest liturgical experiments, the excellence of the 1662 book became an open question. If others could improve on archaic language and redress an inadequate emphasis on thanksgiving, why not Evangelicals? If others could compose family services with evangelistic intent, why not Evangelicals? And once it is conceded that there are inadequacies in the 1662 rite, what biblical or commonsense reason is there for insisting on conformity to one pattern of worship throughout the country?

The same process happened, and is still happening, in the field of church unity. Evangelicals have fairly steadily opposed an approach to unity which seems to put the historic episcopate on a level with the truth of the biblical Gospel, but once it is conceded that the Church as established by the 1662 Act of Uniformity is not the most satisfactory basis for unity today, the essence of the Anglican position comes up for consideration. What does the Church of England stand for in Evangelical eyes if it is not an impeccable doctrinal basis and scriptural worship? The determining principle must be sought out. Some find that the principle is that of reformed catholicism, the kind of position adopted by Colet and More, though sharpened by a better understanding of the cardinal doctrine of justification by faith alone. This makes for attachment to the historic continuing principle which is consistent with such Church of England practices as infant baptism, confirmation and the use of the ring in marriage. It also suggests that such doubtful trappings as "lord" bishops and identification with the Crown can well be lost in the interests of bringing into being an international Church true to the principle of reformed catholicism and free from the local, national aberrations which mar the application of the principle in the Church of England today.

What is true of prayer book revision and church unity is true in other fields. Evangelicals are being compelled to re-examine a number of points which had for reasons satisfactory and unsatisfactory long been closed. This is to say no more than that Evangelicals are having to do what all Christians are having to do. But there is a difference: Evangelicals are themselves changing as they reopen closed issues and measure their accustomed views against Scripture. The limits of Evangelicalism are being much more carefully and precisely examined than has been the case for a very long time.

The spread of Evangelicalism, then, is extensive. At one end of the scale are clergymen with views scarcely distinguishable from those of the Strict Baptists and an allegiance to the Church of England determined presumably solely by the acceptable nature of its formularies. At the other end of the scale are clergymen who have had the authentic Evangelical experience and who hold a view of the authority of Scripture that is different from that of the mainstream Evangelicals. In the middle are those who believe that Evangelical doctrine is consistent with membership of the historic Church—even if that Church does not in every respect measure itself against the Word of God, the Bible. It is this middle group which is committed to an exploration of reformed catholicism.

CHAPTER SEVEN

All Evangelicals are equal but . . .

Amongst the undoubted Evangelicals are many varia-
tions, some blindingly obvious, some subtle. It is not
only important to know whether a person is a true blue
Evangelical; it is important to know what kind of
Evangelical he is. There are many kinds to choose from.
Some are described below.

First we may mention the I V F type. This is a type
of Evangelicalism that emerged between the two world
wars as a result of a bid for intellectual respectability on
the part of a group that has traditionally favoured warm
hearts above clear heads. The Inter-Varsity Fellowship
now occupies what may fairly be described as the
citadel of Evangelical orthodoxy; its basis of faith is
precise and forms an imperial yardstick of sound
Evangelical doctrine. The I V F has considerably influenced Evangelicals within the Church of England.

The influence of the I V F is strong because it cap-
tures the minds of students. It has imparted a new
twist to Evangelical religion. Sound doctrine has been
preserved at the cost of quenching adventurous spirits,
and an intellectual content has been imparted to the

faith. So well has this been imparted that it is now hardly noticed that the Gospel has been over-intellectualised and consequently insulated from the market-place.

The Christian Unions (the I V F organisations in universities and colleges) shape Christianity by force of example. A man who has belonged to a C U during his university or college days has (particularly if the C U gave him his introduction to the Christian faith) been strongly influenced by a form of Christianity that has little room for the sacraments and the doctrine of the Church. Baptism and the Lord's Supper are put on one side in a C U, and it is a standing temptation to the C U member subsequently to leave them on one side. If a Christian fellowship can function adequately without the Lord's Supper, what consideration can make it of first importance (compared, for example, with the prayer meeting) in later life? The I V F influence operates in fact by fostering artificial communities and a simplified version of Christianity.

Another determining factor in the Evangelical movement is the "Bash camp" group. This, like other determining factors, developed its full powers between the wars. Its founder was the Rev E. J. H. Nash (hence the "Bash") and its influence was directed at schoolboys at a select list of boarding-schools. Summer camps were its chief weapons. Many leading Evangelicals today would say that their Christian faith is due to "Bash".

The characteristics of the "Bash camp" movement

are striking. Its followers are devotionally disciplined (whatever else has to go, their morning "quiet time" is never missed), deferential to the Establishment (the movement depended for its success on gaining a good reputation among headmasters and parents), and dedicated to mutual loyalty. Many "Bash campers" went from school to Cambridge and became pillars of the Cambridge Inter-Collegiate Christian Union, so that it was possible when the movement was at its zenith for a boy to go from public school to Cambridge, to ordination, to a curacy and to a parish of his own without having encountered the kind of life lived outside those particular circles.

Much of the present leadership among Evangelicals comes from the "Bash camp" movement, and an understanding of it is essential for the person wishing to know how the Evangelical mind works. Controversy is eschewed by "Bash campers"; it is held to be noisy and undignified—and potentially damaging. As a result many issues which ought to be faced are quietly avoided. Any practical decisions that must be made are taken discreetly by the leadership and passed down the line. The loyalty of the rank and file is such that decisions are respected; any who question are liable to find themselves outside the pale.

If the "Bash camp" movement must be summed up in a word, it must be said that it is too spiritual. Like the I V F, it is based on an over-simplification. It does not give a place to the processes of argument, consultation and independent thought which are essential to any genuine co-operation, inside the Church or outside it. While the structure of the Church of England remained as stable as the Rock of Gibraltar, such an attitude was effective enough; it meant that there were clergymen devotedly and spiritually working through the existing system to bring the A B C of the Gospel to the English people. But when the structure came under examination and amendment was in the air, a more thoroughgoing approach was required; and for this something different from the regimental loyalty of the subaltern was required.

At the opposite extreme to the "Bash campers" are the Evangelical politicians. The "Bash camper" characteristically suspects and deplores church politics — probably because he has not defined his terms sufficiently clearly. Politics, within the Church or outside it, is not essentially a dirty business, a matter of horse-trading, back-scratching and shady compromise; it is the process by which things get done in any society. Politics is therefore what you make it—honest discussion and the formation of parties to achieve particular ends by recognised means (usually the vote)—or a matter of intrigue, backstairs influence and the old pals' act. Politics will inevitably involve compromise (the kind of compromise that was necessary to get the Keele statement accepted, for example), but it is quite unrealistic to expect any society (the Church, the State or the Evangelicals within the Church of England) to organise itself without politics. The only question is: what kind of politics are you going to have?

Evangelical politicians are stronger in the House of Laity than amongst the clergy. The lay representatives get their teeth into votes, resolutions, amendments and committees and win the best kind of bargain they can. By comparison the Church of England Evangelical Council (ostensibly designed to advance Evangelical interests) is a collection of idealists; it rates its own unity higher than realistic policies and is not prepared to use necessary means to achieve the ends it desires. Its strongest move is to issue a statement; in its tiny way it resembles the United Nations Organisation in being an impotent talking-shop.

The C P–A S type is in its own way as identifiable as the I V F type. C P–A S stands for Church Pastoral-Aid Society and operates exclusively within the Church of England. It sets itself to support the work of the Church of England through its existing system, and is therefore a firm supporter of the parochial system, patronage, monarchical ministry and all the other familiar features of the Church of England landscape. Support is given by means of grants to pay curates' salaries; these grants were in former years rather more important than they are today. Increasing diocesan quotas and the corresponding strengthening of the official machinery *vis-à-vis* the voluntary societies have made C P–A S grants more nearly marginal.

C P–A S is penny-plain. The parishes on its network

(grant-aided, under the direct or indirect patronage of
C P–A S, or supporters of the society) are characteristically plodding and conventional. Many are down-
town. At the annual tea for C P–A S clergymen and
women workers, sports jackets and flannel trousers are
in evidence. C P–A S incumbents tend to be worthy
but dull. C P–A S churches tend to have colourless
interiors. C P–A S annual meetings tend to be the same
from year to year and, like the annual reports, to
feature encouraging snippets "from a northern incumbent", or "a grantee curate in the West of England".

C P–A S has considerable influence. It gives back-
bone to Church of England Evangelicals and provides
a nervous system to keep them in touch. Its organising
secretaries are consultants, guides and friends to the
parishes in their areas. C P–A S reinforces the *status
quo* by its loyalty to the present system, whatever its
defects, and its refusal to take any prominent part in
arguing out the case for or against parochial reform. Its
annual sermons are unexceptionable. Its insistence
(more or less universal until recently) that clergymen
helped by the society shall stand sideways at the Communion service has provided a touchstone by which a
man's true blue Evangelicalism can be recognised, but
it is a touchstone which has little relevance today, now
that no particular stance is prescribed in *Second Series*.
Forty years ago it was a useful means of distinguishing
1662 loyalists from 1928 hotheads, but its retention
today, when the westward position is widely acceptable

and churches are being built for congregational worship rather than as medieval replicas, is of dubious value. It is a factor in fossilising worship, and it will be a sign that Evangelicalism is ready for new things when the north side rule is honoured in the breach more than it already is.

A newcomer to the scene is the "tongues" enthusiast. Membership of this movement is not restricted to Evangelicals, but its main support probably comes from them. The "tongues" enthusiast may be interested in Anglican–Methodist unity, synodical government, etc, but his main concern is that the Church should recover the power of the Holy Spirit, and this, he believes, is evidenced by the gifts of the Spirit (by which he means "tongues", "healing", etc).

The influence of the "tongues" movement may be regarded as a counter-poise to the intellectualised tradition fostered by the I V F. Instead of sharp definitions and crystal-clear statements of doctrine, the ruling principle is life, wherever it may be found. A key figure in the movement is the Rev Michael Harper, a Church of England clergyman. The movement has fired many with enthusiasm and has divided more than one parish into opposed groups of adherents and non-adherents.

A similar tight-knit group within Church of England Evangelicalism is the Ruanda movement. This consists of people influenced by the East African revival movement, through the Ruanda Mission. It has been in the field longer than the "tongues" enthusiasts. When it first gained supporters widely in this country, soon after the 1939–45 war, it was marked by mutual confession of sins—resentment, sexual shortcomings, vanity, etc— but this is not so evident now. Its main emphasis, however, is as strong as ever, an insistence that the Christian must be "broken" if the power of Christ is to be seen in his life. "Not I but Christ" is the slogan, and it is interpreted as an end to the proud, self-sufficient, erect capital "I" and a place for the bowed, humbled, "broken" believer symbolised by the letter "C". Nobody who has known the movement can deny that its followers are sincere Christians looking for the best way to serve Christ. They demonstrate a humility which is welcome and delightful in this pushing age. But it must be said that like all recipes for instant holiness, the Ruanda "message" is unsatisfactory. It does not produce balanced Christians; it produces self-effacing, shrinking, diffident men and women—and this is manifestly not the prevailing type of Christian character in the New Testament. "Brokenness" is not a sufficient solution to all problems; it puts energy, enthusiasm and the proper development of personality at a discount. Had Luther been influenced by the Ruanda movement there would never have been a Protestant Reformation; had St Paul been influenced by it, there would never have been the letter to the Galatians.

Other elements in the Evangelical spectrum abound. There are the blinkered Protestants who think all would be well if only people would stick to the 1662 prayer book (well, most of it) and make sure that all those clergymen who could not subscribe wholeheartedly to the Thirty-nine Articles (well, most of them) were thrown out. There are the fervid Sabbatarians who exalt the Sabbath to the same heights as do the Seventh-Day Adventists (but do not show the same logic as the S D As in observing it on Saturday). There are the neo-Puritans who devour the works of Baxter, Charnock, Gurnall and Owen and speak of mortification, practical holiness and perseverance. Neo-Puritans are not admirers of another element in the spectrum, the Keswick Convention, but both agree in their enthusiasm for inter-Church conferences. The Keswick conventioneers meet in the summer, the Neo-Puritans in the winter.

CHAPTER EIGHT

Adolescent Christianity?

One matter that demands explanation is the presence in the Church of England of many erstwhile Evangelicals who are now anything but Evangelical. Sometimes they look back wryly to what they consider to have been their naïve days of youthful enthusiasm; sometimes they have developed a warm animosity towards those who, as it now appears to them, hookwinked them into a particular brand of Christianity under false pretences. Sometimes there is a note, almost of regret, at the passing of the dear dead days which are gone beyond recall.

Is Evangelicalism a mere stage on the journey? Is it a phase through which adolescents characteristically pass? It can scarcely be doubted that Evangelicalism makes a great appeal to young people. It is clear-cut; it demands a definite and often sacrificial response; it moulds strong conformist groups within which the inadequate can feel secure. More than this, it is a form of religion which young people sometimes seek to preserve when they leave the university or college where their C U connection had singular importance. It *can* be a severe shock for a young person who has enjoyed the companionship of talented C U members to come to terms with the stodgy, rut-ridden, mixed group who form the local church which he finds when he leaves the university. In the face of this it is not surprising that young Christians—especially if they first come into a Christian experience at the university—should endeavour to perpetuate the kind of Christian society that they knew in the palmy days. This leads to the phenomenon of the perpetual adolescent, the hearty ex-C U member who, despite his family, mortgage, garden and family responsibilities, is still no more than the young man he was at the university.

It is idle to pretend that C U-type Christianity is suitable fare for the adult. It is basic Christianity that has been simplified and pre-digested for consumption by beginners. That it is this kind of thing reflects no discredit upon it. After all, basic Christianity is better than no Christianity at all, and this is all too often the only other choice before us. For all its faults, C U-type Christianity is a vital, meaningful thing; it fosters lay responsibility, for example, to a degree that is unknown in the average local church.

But the C U is not and cannot be a Church, and because it cannot be this it cannot be free to follow the New Testament pattern. A Christian Union does not administer baptism or the Lord's Supper; it puts the doctrine of the Church on one side; it restricts its interests to its own clearly defined programme and carries on its activities as though other pressing

Christian concerns were of no consequence. For those who understand that a C U is a temporary association, formed for a specific, limited purpose, in which Christians who already have a church loyalty engage because, amongst other things, they wish to forward this specific limited service, all is well. But for those who get the impression that C U life and activity is the exemplar upon which all subsequent church life should be modelled, there are unhappy results. No local church can provide the glitter and diversity of a university junior common room; no local church can ignore the sacraments; no local church can turn a blind eye to the Church at large. In an everyday context the simplified Christianity of the C U is seen to be over-simplified, painfully basic, unacceptably pre-digested.

To put it another way, there is often a touch of the provincial about Evangelicalism. It makes discoveries (about aspects of secularisation, for example, as it did at Keele in 1967) and whoops with delight—forgetting that more cosmopolitan Christians (those who read Harvey Cox and Charles Davis, for example) had their eyes opened to these things years ago. By restricting reading lists to books by other Evangelicals the provincialism is maintained; unorthodox ideas do not get through. This provincialism is embarrassing to the Evangelical who knows that 39, Bedford Square and 7, Wine Office Court do not have the answers to all our problems; it is one of the factors which make intelligent, open-minded Evangelicals footloose.

E

Evangelicalism is (to the outsider) unbelievably patriarchal, and this accentuates its adolescent character. A handful of senior Evangelicals are regarded with a deference that amounts almost to awe. Their theology is impeccable (and the conservating function is peculiarly prestigious among Evangelicals) and they are looked upon as trustees or guardians without whose approval no enterprise can fitly be undertaken. And, let there be no doubt, they are gifted, dedicated men with an unquenchable desire to serve Christ and his Gospel. But upon their shoulders has been laid a burden more than any man should carry. It is they who, probably without adequate ground-level experience, find themselves expected to say yes or no to propositions thrown up by young admirers. The process is not explicit; there is no formal channel of communication; but the Evangelical network is close-meshed, and the brave young pioneer soon discovers that his efforts have the approval or otherwise of his seniors. An Evangelical who speaks out of turn finds he has committed a heinous offence. A pained look and the implication that he has let the side down, rocked the boat, or caused division in the camp are his reward. If his offence has been flagrant, he may find that he receives a rebuke from a custodian.

One of the characteristics of the mature man (and it applies equally well to the Christian and non-Christian alike) is an independent mind. Charles Simeon recognised this when he prescribed that any new member of his trust should be "a truly pious and devoted man, a man of God in deed and in truth, who with his piety combines a solid judgment and a perfectly independent mind". Evangelicalism, it can fairly be said, encourages conformism rather than creativity, assent rather than initiative. Enthusiasm must be directed along carefully marked channels. Soundness, rather than diversity, is the *summum bonum*. As a means of drilling youngsters in rudimentary religion this is possibly an acceptable method. After all, the prayer book catechism sets out with something like the same goal in mind. But for the man bearing responsibilities, for the man having to make a choice which will affect the lives of other people, this kind of religious training is irrelevant. It is like expecting a child who has been drilled in clause-analysis to be able to write persuasive prose without systematic exercise in putting his theoretical knowledge to work.

Undoubtedly Evangelical religion has been deeply influenced by the keenly felt need to make the Christian faith intelligible and palatable to the child. The expertise of the Scripture Union in this field—and particularly its diversification since the war—is a good example of the care that has gone into this activity. But the very excellence of the achievement has misled its supporters; it has been concluded that what is appropriate and effective for the child is sufficient to satisfy the adult.

It does not quite work out that way. The man entering into middle age finds that his rudimentary religious faith does not match his day-to-day commitments. He has the responsibility of increasing sales, or entertaining prospective clients, or coming to terms with union demands, or fighting for his department in a board meeting. He bumps hard into the problems of diffused responsibility, of muddle and laziness which jeopardise the willingness of conscientious men, of the need to get the best bargain he can, of corporate guilt—and the A B C outlines of individual piety do not help him with these problems. (It must of course be recognised that he would find plenty of help in these matters if he read the Bible for himself without obliterating all consciousness of day-to-day happenings.)

Men of independent mind discover in fact that to be a Christian is not merely to read your Bible and pray every day, to go to church on Sundays and to attempt to bring other people to Christ. To be a Christian is to discharge your primary responsibilities in a way that pleases God. This, in a fallen, muddled world, is a supremely difficult task. The matter of finding the will of God is almost as difficult as actually doing it, despite what pietists may say. Evangelical religion often becomes an artificial exercise unrelated to the actual demands of life. One's Christian life is put into a department of its own, with its own tasks, its own conventions, its own ideals. The actual business of living goes on alongside. This is the kind of dichotomy that, in extreme cases, can lead men into the grossest hypocrisy, and more often can lead them into an affable pietism.

Evangelicals fail to achieve the rich diversity that is displayed by independent men of other convictions; their goal is conformity and they tend therefore to spend their energies on being like others rather than on carving their own ideas out of the raw stuff of life. This makes for dullness. It also makes for a departure from Evangelicalism when a man slowly begins to think for himself and develop ideas at variance with the received Evangelical notions. It should not be necessary for a man to think that he must cease being an Evangelical if he likes the occasional pint of bitter, if he likes colourful church interiors, if he is a pacifist, or an admirer of William Golding's novels, but such is the cohesion of Evangelical community life that he can feel very much like a man sent to Coventry if he develops ideas at odds with those of his brethren on subjects like these.

Conformity in these particular social and peripheral matters is achieved only by a process of repressing genuine convictions; it takes the stuffing out of men. The man who finds this process irksome gets on with things in his own way and probably stops being an Evangelical. The man who stays and conforms helps to ensure that Evangelicalism never rises above the mediocre.

One cannot avoid asking whether Evangelicalism has developed into a closed system of the kind Arthur Koestler describes in *Arrow in the Blue* (Collins).

Koestler suggests three characteristics of the closed system: a comprehensive way of looking at life which claims to solve all problems and right all wrongs; the fact that a closed system will not allow itself to be modified by newly observed facts but will absorb the impact of those facts by well-developed casuistry; and the fact that critical faculties are disarmed once the initiate has stepped inside the system. To some extent Evangelicalism does show these characteristics. It has an apostolic hierarchy, with an inner caucus preserving the traditional shape of Evangelicalism. There is the emotional heat which turns disagreements into betrayals and heresies; there is the patient tolerance shown by the insiders to those still outside; they, poor chaps, just cannot understand, and how could they be expected to?

If Koestler's three characteristics can in some measure be found amongst Evangelicals, it must be pointed out that from time to time one comes across the young Evangelical layman whose independence of mind has been fostered in his home, his school or his business life and is slow to wither inside a religious society. He may well smoke a pipe (thereby breaking a taboo) and speak in a cavalier way of the damage done by Christian missionaries in Wagga-Wagga land (thereby showing that he retains his critical faculties). He may express disappointment with sermons which labour the need for conversion while neglecting to speak precisely and practically on urgent issues confronting lay people (and he will thereby show that he does not gullibly accept the values that the hierarchy have approved for general distribution). The strange thing about meeting such a man is that he seems like a Protestant among pre-Reformation Catholics; he is thinking for himself and has no qualms about doing so, despite the fears of his more conservative friends.

An authoritarian system, whatever it is, badly needs men of independent mind if its members are not to become supine or arrogant. A good test of Evangelical religion is whether it is producing many men of this kind.

In sum, Evangelicalism as we know it at present is a little too inbred, a little too timid about taking risks, a little too anxious to avoid a rift in the lute, a little too *safe* to be equal to the needs of the adult Christian. The man who wants to experiment, to pioneer, to come up with answers that have not been pre-judged finds the restrictions irksome and goes off to work things out for himself outside Evangelicalism.

CHAPTER NINE

Mr Obsolete, Mr Go-ahead and Mr Ill-at-ease

When Bunyan's pilgrim was undertaking his journey, he fell in with such characters as Watchful, Mistrust and Timorous. The pilgrim who goes from one Evangelical church to another today is likely to meet Mr Obsolete, Mr Go-ahead and Mr Ill-at-ease. Mr Obsolete favours a style of religion admirably adapted to the needs of nineteenth-century middle-class churchgoers. Mr Go-ahead is always adopting new measures to make Christianity meaningful to non-churchgoers; and Mr Ill-at-ease does his best in a situation which, it seems, was never envisaged when Evangelicalism was invented.

Mr Obsolete makes it his aim to bring individual men to a knowledge of salvation. It is he who has made it possible for Evangelicalism to be labelled as individualistic. His entire parish programme is designed to secure conversions. Every contact has an ulterior (though hardly culpable) motive. Mr Obsolete is not interested in making changes in institutions because he does not recognise that they have any power to shape the men who belong to them. He preaches long sermons because he believes that a lengthy address directed at rows of silent listeners in a church building is God's appointed way of turning non-Christians into Christians. Here or there one or two will respond and this will justify the labour. The pulpit is the focal point of his ministry; and his ministry is the task of gathering in, one by one, those people whom God has pre-selected to be saved.

Mr Obsolete demonstrates his belief in a Gospel of individualism most clearly by his support of mass crusades. This, he thinks, is the most effective type of evangelism because it brings the largest number of individuals within range of a trusted preacher.

Mr Obsolete is keen on Sunday schools because they provide a means of putting across the Christian message to children who would otherwise not hear it. Mr Obsolete is not very impressed by the arguments of those who say that the family and the school are the principal places in which a child should be instructed; he has little interest in the training of children within the family, and he is suspicious of the kind of teaching that may be given in school. He therefore prefers Sunday schools staffed by well-meaning amateurs and attended by children of parents who are indifferent about the religious education of their children.

Mr Obsolete has come to have a distorted view of Scripture. He forgets that great areas of church life are omitted from the New Testament record, and he blurs his own traditional understanding into what is actually found in the text. Thus, he is quite convinced that entirely predictable forms of worship are perfectly in harmony with the New Testament (despite I Corinthians 14), and he overlooks the fact that in New Testament days preaching was, as often as not, a matter of calling a noisy open-air crowd to order so as to tell them something they had never heard before. Mr Obsolete has allowed himself to be convinced that it is only the actual word "Parliament" that is missing from the passages that suggest to him that the Church should receive its doctrine and its chief officers from the State.

Mr Obsolete has a scanty awareness of the world to-day. It is of little interest to him that he lives in a bustling, questioning, inquisitive society that ignores the Churches but buys religious books. He would look at you blankly if you told him that his contemporaries demonstrate their deep concern about the human predicament by the plays they watch and the marches they join. His preaching is what it was thirty years ago. The world has moved on, but he has not understood that this is so.

Mr Go-ahead is always breaking new ground. In his family services he uses *Contemporary Prayers for Public Worship*. In his visiting he recommends Alan Dale's *New World* to people who think the New Testament is a dull book. Mr Go-ahead accepts that the responsibility is his when people say that they cannot understand religion or that they find it wearisome. Instead of grumbling at non-churchgoers (or scolding vicariously those who do come) he tries to get inside their minds to see why they do not come; he is ready to believe that the fault may lie with the churchgoers, and mostly with himself.

Mr Go-ahead knows that the sermon is an extremely inefficient teaching method and is well aware that if he conducted a written test among his congregation on basic knowledge of the Bible, for example, the results would probably be deplorable. He is also aware that if an honest discussion took place on how much of the Apostles' Creed the members of the congregation actually believe, the opinions would vary a good deal. So, whenever he has the opportunity, Mr Go-ahead uses diagrams, runs competitions and invites comment so that differences and difficulties can be brought into the open and dealt with effectively.

Mr Go-ahead is prepared to learn from such people as Harvey Cox, Leslie Paul and Eric James. He recognises that there is much he does not know about urban communities today and he is prepared to learn from others. He is also prepared to be unconventional.

Remembering that he has more security than the people he is preaching to (although his income may be small it is just about 100 per cent secure, and so is the roof over his head), Mr Go-ahead is diffident about urging his hearers to venture out in faith and put safety last in life. He knows that he is scarcely in a position to talk about faith in practical terms like this while he is enjoying his unassailable parson's freehold.

One of Mr Go-ahead's most endearing character-istics is his readiness to measure accepted patterns against Scripture—to allow his Evangelicalism to be true to itself, in other words. He has an open mind about indiscriminate baptism, for example, and he is open to new ideas about church architecture. He thinks for himself about women's ministry. If Christians out-side the Church of England have discovered new ways that are better than his, he considers those ways and seeks to get them adopted.

Mr Go-ahead is keen on decontaminating over-intellectualised Christianity. He knows that Christianity was intended not only for graduates and contro-versialists; in the time of Christ it made its strongest appeal to the ordinary people. When ordinary people pay no attention to Christianity Mr Go-ahead suspects that it may be that something is wrong with the Churches rather than with the ordinary people. He is prepared to meet people in their homes and answer the questions they are actually asking rather than preach week after week to the converted. Mr Go-ahead, in short, is good at *listening*.

Mr Ill-at-ease is a plodder. He conscientiously does what he believes to be his duty, but he sometimes wonders whether he is going the right way about it. He prepares sermons, addresses women's meetings, attends committees, orders coke, but occasionally a slight doubt as to whether this is the kind of thing for which he was ordained enters his mind.

Mr Ill-at-ease quenches his doubts, however. He is doing the kind of work, running the kind of parish programme, preaching the kind of sermons that all his friends approve. Mr Ill-at-ease, remember, belongs to a tight-knit association. The grapevine rapidly transmits information and labels. Pressure towards conformity is marked. Fear of being thought unorthodox cramps many a parochial programme. If your friends are waiting to dub you "unsound" the moment you allow your people a free vote on dancing or drama, you are hesitant about taking a step that would put you beyond the pale. Mr Ill-at-ease never takes such a step.

Mr Ill-at-ease feels the burden of responsibility for biblical Christianity weighing heavily upon his shoulders. He sees himself as the custodian of received Evangelical values in his locality. He must at all costs preserve the deposit. The result is a one-man band. Instead of a meeting of minds and some degree of consensus in parish policy there is something not far removed from a vicar's *fiat*; Mr Ill-at-ease almost unconsciously reserves policies and aims to himself. If members of his P C C, for example, are not committed Evangelicals, he opens only part of his mind and confidence, and works for the day when all the key positions in the church are occupied by those who share his theological convictions. His long-term aim is a take-over, a take-over that will, he believes, turn the parish

into a pulsating centre of Christianity. Mr Ill-at-ease
has never a qualm as to whether such tactics are appropriate in an established Church designed to comprehend
as many Christians as possible.

A friend may one day ask Mr Ill-at-ease whether it is
right, for example, to proscribe drama and dancing in
the parish by a mere vicar's say-so—and to back up the
edict by an implicit threat of resignation if the decision
is not respected. Is this the kind of way, he may go on
to ask, to promote lay responsibility? Mr Ill-at-ease is
shaken but unyielding. He *knows* that the policy he is
following is the best for his parishioners. The alternative is to take risks, to give unenlightened and half-
convinced lay people the responsibility of making a
decision themselves. But to take such a risk may expose
Mr Ill-at-ease to the charge of tolerating "worldly"
activities—and such a charge is a damaging one in the
Evangelical world, almost as damaging as compromis-
ing over costume in church services.

Mr Obsolete, Mr Go-ahead and Mr Ill-at-ease
would plainly find it helpful to discuss things together.
They all claim to be ready to shape their convictions
and methods according to Scripture, but they are poles
apart and there is a mutual suspicion that can scarcely
be overcome until the underlying attitudes are put into
words and argued out thoroughly and charitably. The
unity that exists among these representatives of differing Evangelical outlooks is in fact specious; it is little
more than a cosy *camaraderie* depending upon the

suppression of controversial issues. It is also slightly paranoid and regressive. A discussion would be useful. But if these three are to talk together honestly, then there must be a greater readiness than hitherto to call things by their proper names and to recognise that more than one Evangelical opinion is possible. It must also be conceded that prevailing patterns of Evangelicalism may be less than the best.

CHAPTER TEN

Blind spots

Like every other version of Christianity, Evangelicalism has its blind spots. Though it may fancy itself exempt from shortcomings painfully apparent in forms of Christianity ostensibly giving less respect to the Bible, it nevertheless stands condemned at many points when measured against New Testament principles. The best of us see only in part, and it needs to be said that Evangelicals have not been given answers to problems that have been insoluble since time began and will remain insoluble until we see things fully in the light of glory.

Blind spots there are, and distortions too. Accepting the sovereignty of Scripture as a determining principle is no guarantee that sensible conclusions will be drawn; neither is it a guarantee that those accepting the principle will be realistic and widely experienced. Like other men, Evangelicals are subject to timidity and gregariousness; they are also prone to self-deception.

It is easy to understand objections to eucharistic vestments which have an indelible association with the medieval Mass, but it is less easy to understand a repudiation of any attempt to advertise the particular stage of the Church calendar by colour variations at such focal points as the Communion Table, the lectern and the pulpit. One of the most encouraging signs of creativity in Evangelical worship will be a readiness to design and use entirely new costumes in church (and, incidentally, in everyday life).

So far little that is good and creative has been forthcoming from Evangelicals in the field of church architecture. St Barnabas, Cray, Kent, is an honest building, functionally designed; so is St Mary, Peckham, London. But numerous Evangelical church buildings are a sad commentary on the lifeless imitation of medieval models which has prevailed in the Church of England at large for too long. Architects have evidently been briefed without any determined exploration of what is actually being done elsewhere and what is actually possible today. The result all too often is an unimaginative building (perhaps with a gimmick or two) which does indeed accommodate worshippers and keep them dry but which fails to make a Christian statement and fails to encourage its users to worship as a redeemed fellowship.

Colourless church interiors are one blind spot. There *are* Evangelical churches where colour—even garish colour—stuns the visitor. Hamworthy parish church, Dorset, is one such church. But more often than not drabness prevails. Like the preference for magpie ministers in surplice and scarf (though, strangely enough,

F

degree hoods are allowed to brighten the costume), the uninteresting nature of Evangelical church interiors is determined by a reaction against images, elaborate vestments and architectural exuberance. Rationalised as a reluctance to spend money on expensive ornamentation, it is symptomatic of the negative reaction that can make religion a cramping, sensibility-crushing process.

Sometimes the shrinking from colour is turned into a virtue, and styled simplicity. Respect for simplicity is something that should never be discounted, but simplicity is order and clarity, and order and clarity are frequently the very qualities which are conspicuously absent from church interiors. The furniture clutters and crowds; nothing is predominant and accentuated; all is lost in a welter of pews, cheap and nasty woodwork, crude encaustic tiles and hideous carpets.

With colour-blindness and lack of design-consciousness goes a depraved taste in music and verse. Choruses and hymns with sickly-sweet music are sung on church premises; doggerel is quoted in sermons and parish magazines. The fibreless words and music are significant not only as instances of poor taste and lack of critical integrity; they are also symptomatic of superficiality and an unhappy tendency to trivialise.

Evangelicals have not for many years made a noticeable contribution to the arts, either as creators or critics. Why this should be so is a fascinating subject for inquiry; it is doubtless connected with the utilitarian theology, as it were, of the best of the Puritans, with the debased Puritan tradition that failed to appreciate the function of the imagination, with the preponderance of a Plymouth Brother, Schofield Bible, crude mission-hall type of Christianity that was as far removed from the Romantic movement and the Oxford Movement as it was possible to get. Whatever the reason, Evangelicals were, between the wars, anti-theatre, anti-novel, anti-any serious art form. The head and front of the offence was the cinema. Young people were taught to think that a visit to a cinema was the first step to apostasy. "Worldliness" was a matter of flagrant breaches of a tried and proven scheme for Christian development, and the cinema was a synagogue of Satan. The inevitable result followed. The good was proscribed along with the bad. Christian young people failed to develop powers of judgment in relation to a prevailing art form, and any positive contribution that might have been forthcoming was stultified by a negative and censorious tradition that interpreted Christianity as a personal code in which Safety First was a prominent feature.

The situation now is different. Television turned the flank. Elderly Evangelicals who before the war would never have been seen entering a cinema were found soon after the war basking before a television screen. Articulate young people began to point out that the negative tradition was inadequate and dangerous. If Evangelicalism has not yet produced its own Harold Pinter or Robert Bolt, it has produced a generation which can appreciate Pinter and can express appropriate contempt for crass propaganda which is dully orthodox and impeccably useless.

A side-effect of the Safety First attitude to the arts has been the emergence of a humourless type of character. Not as pronounced as that satirised by Ben Jonson, it is none the less naïve and suspicious of wit. An editor of *Inter-Varsity* (the I V F magazine) once found that an invitation to readers to contribute verse on the chief failings of Evangelicals produced a painfully worded reaction from a senior and much respected Evangelical leader. Evangelicals, he said, were precious in the sight of God and not to be mocked. The tortuous self-explanation that precedes an attempt by a leader to take a new line (like commitment to "ecumenical dialogue", or to an examination of issues actually before Christians today instead of more and more Bible study) is an example of the habit of taking oneself more seriously than one ought.

This humourless outlook is not perhaps so serious as outright hypocrisy or a cloud of cant, but it distorts the Christian character and makes it difficult for any writer who wishes to depart from the wordy tracts of prose generally regarded as appropriate. To write with one's tongue in one's cheek, for example, is to invite trouble; readers simply will not understand.

Coupled with repudiation of the arts goes an exaggerated respect for economic and other similar virtues. After all, if you are going to cut out much that makes life worth living, you must fill it with something else.

So it happens that young Evangelicals have traditionally been absent from dramatic groups and present on
the cricket, rugger and hockey fields. Athletic prowess
is acceptable. And not only acceptable, admirable. For
success as a sportsman may ensure a hearing for the
message. What is true of sport is true of making money.
The Christian must be a worker. This was put in its
harshest terms by Fred Catherwood when he wrote in
an article in *Inter-Varsity*: "Christianity knows nothing of an ideal of leisure or contemplation." Other
Christians leaped to repudiate this view, but the fact
that it could be expressed at all shows how easily the
economic virtues—thrift, application, industry, etc.—
can make nonsense of the scale of values implied in
Philippians 4 : 8 and Matthew 6 : 24–34. It is a short
step from this exaltation of economic virtues to a position in which productivity is a god. It is a short step
also to the relegation of faith, hope and love to the tail-
end of the virtues. But there is an encouraging awareness that the admission of the economic virtues in this
way is the admission of a Greek horse into Troy, and
there are Evangelicals today (though it could not be
said that they are in the majority) who know that when
non-Christians show more awareness of the human
predicament and more depth in their treatment of life's
problems than Christians, the time has come for
Christians to abdicate.

A middle-class bias is another blind spot. The
"correspondence" being conducted by David Sheppard

and others working in down-town areas demonstrates that there is a lively concern that Evangelical Christianity should break out of the straitjacket fastened on to it over the years. The matter-of-fact (and Evangelically unorthodox) approach found in numerous down-town parishes in the south and the north is another hopeful sign. But Evangelical Christianity is impeded in its work by the fact that it is tailored to suit the needs of a well-to-do middle class which no longer exists. The strongpoints of Evangelicalism today are found in the comfortable suburbs.

While the Salvation Army and the Roman Catholics have adapted themselves, their devotional practices, their music, and their ministry to the needs of the under-privileged, the Evangelicals have perpetuated patterns which start from the premise that people responding to the Evangelical proclamation of the Gospel are educated, leisured and employed in responsible jobs. Standard devotional forms for personal use (e.g. the daily reading of a Bible passage plus notes) require the type of intellectual application and sustained effort that result (or should result) from a grammar school education. The services and committees of the local church require a similar degree of expertise as the prevailing norm. There is an accompanying implication that Christianity is a leisure-time interest and that Christian enthusiasm is measured by attendance at church meetings. Primary responsibilities—those of the parent, the employee, the citizen—are not regarded as areas in which Christians should find their chief means of expression.

This sociological unawareness has wider consequences. It is not difficult to find a flourishing suburban church bursting at the seams with able workers while a few miles away an inner suburban church is at its last gasp. The two parishes may be obviously adapted to harmonious co-operation, but the sense of responsibility for another part of the city is not part and parcel of Christianity today, as Harvey Cox suggested it ought to be. One outstanding instance where this sense of responsibility is evident and operational is the link between Reigate, Surrey, parish church and St Saviour, Battersea; there could be many more.

A sense of strategy, indeed, is notably lacking amongst Evangelicals. Parishes are watertight units. At all costs an Evangelical succession must be preserved in the ministry. Hence the determined defence of the present patronage arrangements. The total problem of evangelising the English people and Christianising English institutions as a whole is scarcely regarded—or, if it is regarded, nothing is done about it. The preservation of the Evangelical message in all its purity takes precedence over strategic needs and the facts of life today. If an Eric James or a Nicolas Stacey points out that the Church of England is proving ineffective in big cities, the message is not received.

Being a tightly-knit religious club, Evangelicals have little sense of catholicity, history or current problems.

Few Evangelicals are prepared to face the need for compromise implicit in any recognition of non-Evangelicals as Christians. Indeed "compromise" is a dirty word—as it should not be to any Christian seriously considering the Jerusalem Council and Paul's attitude to circumcision. History is similarly of small account. Few Evangelical sermons refer to anything that happened before the Reformation in the British Isles, and there is little readiness to discuss the point that Evangelicalism itself is a phenomenon of recent manifestation.

As far as current problems are concerned, the slogan is: "If it's not in the Bible, it's not important." Allowing the Bible to dictate the agenda, Evangelicals are naïve about such matters as the upbringing of children, the arts, political liberty, crime and punishment. Things would be different if the Bible were regarded as a catalyst, stimulating a reflective and imaginative approach to a variety of matters; when it is regarded as a catalogue, containing a treatment of all the topics a Christian is expected to consider, the effects are unhappy. Christianity gives men new inspiration, a new Spirit, new eagerness to tackle the problems they may encounter; it does not give them a foolproof list of answers to their questions. Only too often Evangelicals have an unimaginative view of the Bible which leads them into trivial opinions on big subjects.

By definition the Evangelicals we are discussing are conservative, conservative in their theology, that is. But they are also conservative in other ways. The conservatism necessary to the preservation of a particular theological view spills over into other departments, so that an Evangelical is likely to take a conservative view of, for example, establishment, or liturgical experiment. Evangelical opponents of the *Series Two* Communion service are sufficiently active to require the Rev K. V. Ensor to send out 600 copies of his duplicated notes attacking the whole conception. It may be said that opposition such as this comes from backwoodsmen, but there is enough weight in it to act as a drag on a group that is reluctant to make policy decisions which would leave less progressive brethren behind. Impatient as the radicals amongst the Evangelicals may be with their reluctant brethren, they have to take account of their views. The Church of England Evangelical Council, for example, has its quota of conservatives and this cramps its style.

Evangelicalism is largely concerned with correctness, and concern for correctness makes for timidity. The extensive doctrinal section of the Keele statement (*Keele '67*, published by C P–A S) betrays a nervous preoccupation with precision in doctrine which makes a noticeable contrast with naïve paragraphs elsewhere. Plainly much more thinking goes on about doctrinal definitions than about making the Gospel meaningful to the people on the housing estate.

The result is that Evangelicals are not the most creative group in the Church of England. Group ministries have been pioneered not by Evangelicals but by others. The Rev Ron Herniman is an Evangelical who has got to grips with the practical issues involved in working an extensive group of parishes in Devon, but his initiative is little known in Evangelical circles, perhaps because he has accepted the need to come to terms with parishioners habituated to different costumes for the clergymen from those which are commonly applauded in Evangelical circles.

As has already been implied, a notable blind spot is "worldliness". It has been accepted by Evangelicals, as it was accepted by those Puritans who incurred Ben Jonson's contempt, that "worldliness" consists in the enjoyment of certain pleasures (hawking, hunting, drinking, dancing—it has varied from one generation to another) and that "worldliness" can be avoided by the simple renunciation of these activities. Such a view is of course extraordinarily naïve; the least experienced man of affairs knows that the spirit of worldliness is seen in the devious, evasive methods of those who achieve their ends by pulling strings, currying favour and tinkering with accepted procedures. Often those who abstain from proscribed pleasures are foremost in using worldly means such as these; they may on the other hand be quite unaware that it is these means which are employed to defend their venerated religious institutions. Often those who practise worldly wiles do so because it is the religious enthusiast who can allow himself to be truly unscrupulous; he is playing for such high stakes that contempt for committees and constitutions seems excusable.

It can happen, of course, that the man who abstains from proscribed pleasures also abstains from political activity within the Church and thereby opts out of what is to many (and understandably so) an unattractive responsibility. Some carry this process further and abstain from almost everything; they live in a religious capsule, having few pleasures and few opportunities of meeting those who do not agree with them. This yearning for total renunciation of "the world" is, however, fading amongst Evangelicals. The renunciation of everything is generally recognised as not only unbiblical but impossible.

CHAPTER ELEVEN

Sacred cows

A sacred cow is different from a blind spot. A blind spot is a failure to notice what is going on in a particular area. A sacred cow is a characteristic pattern of loyalties which has been noticed, rationalised and approved; with the passing of years deep emotions cluster around it and preserve it from objective examination. Blind spots are negative; sacred cows are positive. The remedy for blind spots is an arc light in the hands of an inexorable operator; the remedy for sacred cows is the chopper.

Sacred cows are as prominent a feature of the Evangelical landscape as of any other landscape. They flourish in lush pastures under a patriarchal régime. The 1968 Islington Clerical Conference was interesting because knives were taken to three sacred cows — ivory tower theology, traditional behaviour patterns and clerical domination.

Ivory tower theology is the end-product of an effort to make Evangelicalism intellectually respectable. Theology has been monopolised by a handful of academic clergymen with little parochial experience. The result is an impressive defence of Reformed doctrine, and a capable exposition of that doctrine as applied to ecclesiastical issues—e.g. the Anglican-Methodist unity proposals. Little, however, has been forthcoming of such a character as to have any effect upon missionary and evangelistic strategy in England. Parish and People, the stewardship movement, the liturgical movement and other groups have shown an initiative and adaptability which have had them hurtling along the track while Evangelicals have been stiffly raising themselves off the starting-blocks.

Traditional behaviour patterns form a notable Evangelical sacred cow. An inheritance of taboos laid upon smoking, drinking and theatre-going may seem laughable to people accustomed to making up their own minds about their pleasures, but amongst Evangelicals the inheritance is a formidable one and he is a daring man who refuses to conform. Traditionally it has been accepted that a man who smokes and drinks is a man of little Christian resolution. Yellow finger-tips and a red nose have the merit of being convenient distinguishing features; kindness, patience and love are more elusive qualities. Predictably the problem has been simplified: to be accepted a man must decline alcohol and tobacco, and this despite the fact that the drinking of wine is at the heart of Christian worship. (Caffeine is another matter; in this field, as in the matter of Sabbatarianism, Seventh Day Adventists are more logical in their practice than Evangelicals.)

Little matters like a veneration for ivory tower

theology and a collection of taboos on particular pleasures are harmless enough. The ivory tower theologian is wasting nobody's time but his own, and the man of independent mind can afford to ignore the taboos. It is when the sacred cows crop pastures that should be nourishing the whole Church that they become animals which cannot be afforded. The shape of the ministry as we know it today is one such sacred cow, and it is as sacred to Evangelicals as it is to any other churchmen. The 1968 Islington Conference tilted at clerical domination when it passed a resolution calling for clergymen to give full responsibility to lay people and to diversify ministry, but this resolution was in the event little more than a matter of making the right noises. Evangelical clergymen are simply not prepared to allow lay people to exercise responsibility; it would be too risky. Suppose the lay people voted—as they very likely would—for dancing and play-acting on church premises? The idea, as has been suggested in an earlier chapter, is enough to make a self-respecting Evangelical clergyman wilt with horror—so lay responsibility remains no more than a polite fiction in Evangelical parishes and the monarchical ministry continues, with the vicar acting as preacher, teacher, evangelist, managing director, chairman and chief executive. The monarchical ministry is likely to continue until in the eyes of their clergymen lay people acquire good Evangelical habits.

The present shape of the ministry is therefore a

heavily defended sacred cow. It is a complex formed by the parochial system (i.e. the territorial distribution of clergymen on the lines of one clergyman to each village, as though a clergyman is providing an essential, understood service in the way a doctor does), patronage and a two-level (incumbent and curate) ministry. Evangelicals defend this complex because they are thereby defending the vested interests of Evangelicals, but they lose sight of the fact that what they are defending is an extremely unsatisfactory way of spreading Christianity and a pattern which is contemptuous of the layman's place in the Church.

Nothing reveals the ludicrous nature of the parochial system so clearly as the appointment of young clergymen to be incumbents of mini-parishes (and by the term "mini-parish" is understood a parish with fewer than 1,000 people). Numbers of young vicars and rectors of mini-parishes are giving conscientious service, building up the local church and introducing innovations such as guest services, bookstalls, lay visiting, etc. The incumbents are blameless, or almost so. They responded to God's call to the ministry and now they are serving as opportunity has been given them. But is the Church at large blameless for allowing young men to be given such tiny responsibilities when the needs of urban areas are so great? Can the Church at large expect to be taken seriously when its priorities in deploying highly trained men are so questionable?

It is sometimes said that no clergyman can care for

more than 1,000 people and, that being so, it is as reasonable to place clergymen in the country as in the town; wherever they are, they will be able to contact only a certain number. But if this is so, then nothing would be more reasonable than to start at Land's End and allocate one clergyman to every 1,000 people up through Cornwall, Devon, Somerset and so on until the supply of clergymen ran out somewhere in the west Midlands. It is plainly absurd to appoint clergymen in this way. But it is equally absurd to tolerate gross disparities between the responsibilities of clergymen, so that one is responsible for ten times as many parishioners as another. What would be thought of an educational system that tolerated classes of 35 in one area and classes of 350 in another area? It would be said that immediate changes were necessary. Nothing like this is said, however, about the disposition of clergymen. At least, nothing (or little) is said by Evangelicals. Why not? Because the present arrangements are convenient. The present parochial system retains the loyalty of Evangelicals not because it is an effective, common-sense way of evangelising the English people and providing pastoral care (it is not), but because it is part of the *status quo*; and the *status quo* safeguards the position of Evangelicals.

Independent theological colleges are another sacred cow. It is reasonable for a public school to be governed independently. Other forms of education are available for parents who are not satisfied with the education that is provided by any particular school, and parents are the only people whose interests must be consulted. But a theological college is training ministers for the whole Church, and the kind of training being given in a college is properly the concern of the Church at large. But in practice Evangelicals are foremost in defending the independence of the theological colleges. Why? Because in doing so, they are defending, or think they are defending, the purity of the Gospel. Keep the colleges in trusted hands, it is said, and we can rely upon a succession of Evangelical ministers. So we can. But the present pattern of training for the ministry is, like the parochial system, basically designed for Christian Englishmen living in villages untouched by the Industrial Revolution. While theological colleges remain as they are, we shall continue to train ordinands in the wrong way for the task which will actually confront them. The fact that we shall do the training in an Evangelical way does not excuse the outdated aims. Nonsense is nonsense whether it is Evangelical or otherwise.

To preserve the *status quo* in the theological colleges is to preserve a situation in which a principal and his staff are equivalent to a vicar and his curates in a big old-fashioned parish. The vicar is permanent; curates come and go. The vicar is reasonably paid; the curates are not. The vicar takes the decisions; the curates implement them at his direction. The colleges need a balanced team of senior men who share in the decision-taking.

G

Like other groups, Evangelicals have their pressure groups and vested interests. In a situation where initiative and adaptability are at a premium, it is distressing to have to record that the pressure groups and vested interests are likely to be the result of a response to needs which no longer exist. It is important that Evangelicals should be alert to this danger. Just as generals have frequently wasted their time preparing for the last war when they should have been preparing for the next one, so Evangelicals must ask whether their societies are not wasting their time in the same way. If they are, something should be done about it.

Evangelical societies are very sacred cows. The Keele statement made a tentative reference to them, but the societies have brushed aside any external interest in their own affairs. The societies are not only numerous; they have in some cases aims which are far from clear; they fail to keep in effective touch with their supporters; and they are inadequately representative as far as their committees are concerned—particularly on the lay side. However, like old soldiers, Evangelical societies never die; and even if they show signs of fading away, they still clamour for a place at the conference table.

Sunday observance is another sacred cow. He is a bold Evangelical who will say that the Lord's Day Observance Society is, to put it mildly, on very uncertain ground in its blistering opposition to any liberalising of the English Sunday, yet no Evangelical who takes the New Testament seriously can be a thorough-going Sabbatarian. Christ flouted the careful restrictions placed about the Sabbath by the Pharisees; Paul had little enthusiasm for regarding one day more than another; and the momentous switch of the rest-day from the last to the first day has no specific biblical authority whatever. In the light of these considerations it is at least doubtful whether Sabbatarianism is a live option for a biblical Christian. Yet prominent Evangelicals in the Church of England support the L D O S—and some even contrive at the same time to support such encouragements to Sabbath-breaking and the destruction of the quiet Sunday as a mammoth evangelistic rally in west London. Sunday observance has in fact been too little studied by Evangelicals; the habits that were perhaps sufficient in the days of Bishop Ryle are not adequate to cope with the changes brought about by the motor-car and the television set. If, as some Evangelical leaders say, Sunday is a day when the family should be together, what could be better for the family than a family outing in the car on Sunday afternoon? If Sunday should be restful, what is more restful for the busiest member of the family, mother, than lunch at a hotel in the country?

Sunday schools are another sacred cow. Immense efforts are made to organise Sunday schools attended by children who are enticed into attendance almost without their parents' knowledge or by virtue of the

parents' apathy and desire for a quiet Sunday afternoon. The Sunday school staff have slender qualifica-
tions, if any, for providing a religious education for
children. It can almost be said that instead of reinforc-
ing parental responsibility, which is what Christianity
should do, this pattern is taking advantage of parental
irresponsibility to no clear purpose.

The matter is seen in its proper perspective when
Sunday schools are compared with day schools. L E A
schools still provide a religious education for their
pupils. Christian teachers have the opportunity of giving daily Bible lessons in primary schools and covering
a worthwhile syllabus in secondary schools. Yet young
people who feel, as they say, called to teach remain content to teach for one hour a week in a Sunday school
while they could be teaching for thirty hours a week in
a day school after undergoing a thorough professional
training. It does not make sense to say that you are
called by God to teach if you then teach as little as
possible without the benefit of adequate training.

Sacred cows, it has been said, are preserved from
objective examination (and the chopper) by a cluster of
emotions. It may be worthwhile to look closely at one
sacred cow in an unemotional light.

Our system of appointing the clergy should be based
on principle. This may appear risky—just as it is risky
to revise a prayer book, to give genuine responsibility
to lay people, and (in another context) to give women
the vote—in the eyes of those who are personally satis-

fied with the present arrangements. But respect for principle in such a matter can hardly be denied. What principles, then, should determine our method of appointing the clergy? The following principles are suggested:

1 Spiritually-minded men of independent views must be able to declare the Word of God without fear or favour.

2 The system must command respect.

3 The system must encourage Christian maturity in the clergy.

4 Professional standards must be preserved.

5 The bishop (i.e. the supervisor) must have a proper share of responsibility.

6 The local church (i.e. the lay people) must have a proper share of responsibility.

7 Strategic needs and sociological boundaries must be recognised.

8 Clergymen must not be wasted.

If we measure the present appointments arrangements against these criteria, we find that they fall short in the following respects:

1 The independence of the clergy *is* to some extent preserved, but the parson's freehold has been eroded as the value of his endowments has fallen. It is doubtful whether the type of security offered by the freehold commends the Gospel to people with mortgages and jobs with only ordinary security.

2 Secrecy and non-accountability on the patron's part do not promote confidence.

3 At present clergymen are encouraged to wait for new appointments to drop into their laps. Patrons are encouraged to stand in for God. Clergymen's initiative is discouraged.

4 The solitary deployment of the clergy (together with other factors such as the absence of any rational pay structure) means that they lack inducement to keep up to date professionally.

5 The bishop has no part to play (except where he is patron).

6 The local church (i.e. the lay people) has next to no part to play. Lay people have to accept the vicar chosen for them by somebody else.

7 The present system is inflexible. It does not allow the designation of mission areas (as suggested by the Keele statement), and it pretends that cities are merely villages joined together rather than organic units.

8 Young clergymen *are* wasted.

The Leslie Paul report and the Fenton Morley report point the way to better things, but little progress will be made until it is agreed that only an honest, straightforward and regularised pay structure for the clergy can provide a basis for putting matters right. In this respect the Church must be prepared to take lessons from the teaching profession.

As a short-term measure, great benefit would be derived from the practice of advertising all vacancies. A handful of patrons already advertise their vacancies — e.g. the Hulme Trustees and the Oxford Diocesan Board of Patronage—and invite applications. If this were generally done, new channels would be opened up and no clergyman could say he was forgotten; he could always make application, at least. This would encourage initiative in the clergy.

In the long term the Church of England must collect information and plan its staffing position ahead. This would avoid the scandal of recruiting men for the ministry and having no appropriate jobs to offer them five years after their ordination—a scandal which is not lessened by campaigns to encourage more young men to come forward as ordination candidates. Regional commissions with strong *ad hoc* representation from the parish concerned should make appointments. Lay people would soon develop sufficient resolution to oppose any foolish course urged upon them by their diocesan or regional leaders.

These observations on the appointment of the clergy are based on the fact that we have at present a defective system for deploying our full-time professional ministers. It must be added that we need to reshape our ministry so as to include part-time and voluntary ministers and bring about a situation in which ministry arises as a response to urgent needs. At present we have a ministry, are not sure why we need it and have to think of things for it to do.

CHAPTER TWELVE

Experts on Evangelism?

How much do Evangelicals know about evangelism? It should be the strongest suit in their hands, but in fact it is not. Evangelicals think in terms of getting people to hear sermons (inside church, whereas the apostles preached in the open; in the context of Christian worship, whereas the apostles had to quell riotous crowds bent on mayhem; and one-way whereas the apostles had to deal with heckling and disputatious audiences).

Most people would find it hard to define the word "Evangelical" but those who made the effort would almost inevitably include the word "evangelist" in their definition. Indeed, many would imagine the two to be synonymous. If there is one thing that Evangelicals are believed to be interested in, that thing is evangelism. And this of course is what many hold against them. A naïve, perhaps even overbearing insistence on the necessity of being born again is not by ordinarily educated people today accepted as a substitute for facing facts and thinking logically. At their best Evangelicals do not offer the new birth as a panacea, but Evangelicals, like other people, are not always at their best, and the fact must be faced that to a person who has read D. H. Lawrence for his A levels much Evangelical preaching is thin stuff deserving little attention.

In this matter of evangelism there is no short cut. Christianity survived because it out-thought the best that those of other religious views had to offer. It was a more penetrating analysis of man's condition than the analysis offered by its rivals. These are the terms on which the Christian faith must always fight for a place in the minds of men. The repetition of a few (undoubtedly correct as they may be) phrases does not validate a religious view of life if the phrase-monger is plainly going through life with his eyes shut. The blind cannot lead the blind, no matter how eloquent the blind leader may be on the local topography.

Doubts about mass evangelism are spreading amongst Evangelicals, but there is still enough insistence on this kind of approach to indicate an inadequate understanding of the mass conditioning effect of our architecture, our culture, etc. Men and women do not want to be herded into slab-sided blocks of flats—or vast counselling rooms. Why should they? Why should they be required to go through this mass process to become Christians?

It is sometimes overlooked that *where* and *how* you become a Christian is as important as whether you become a Christian at all. A man who is shaped as a

Christian in a Christian home after being baptised into
Christ as the child of Christian parents is immeasurably
privileged compared with a man who has been hustled
into religious commitment on the basis of an uncertain
grasp of the Gospel and an emphatic call for a verdict
in unfamiliar surroundings which have a conditioning
effect on the strongest temperament. In its way the idea
of drawing people into a crusade meeting is as crude as
the idea of drawing them into a church; both are abrupt,
direct methods which plunge the victim into another
world than the one to which he is accustomed.

The problem of introducing our leisured, contented
(well, fairly) contemporaries to Christ and his Gospel
is a profound one. It is not solved without a determined
effort to put ourselves in the place of the person who is
glad to support Christian Aid but cannot see why the
parish church needs £3,000 for its roof, the Methodist
church is vainly trying to fill its empty pews and a few
hundred yards away the Baptists are busy building a
new church. Often the first step towards effective
evangelism must be some drastic pruning within the
Churches and a realisation that the Churches are only
too often the "religious clubs" described by the Bishop
of Woolwich, cosy groups preoccupied with their own
continued existence and quite out of touch with the
mainstream life of the community round about them.
The non-churchgoer is often a responsible person full
of goodwill to the Churches but unable to take them
very seriously while they perpetuate the fossilised life

which they frequently manifest at the moment. Preaching the Gospel in such a situation can only ever result in a few people responding; on the evidence before him the proclamation is unconvincing.

What is in fact needed more often than not is an indirect method of evangelism—a non-church-based movement like the Stewards' Trust which sets out to put the Gospel on the map in London in the context of expensive hotels and week-end Bible reading parties. Outside the West End the house-meeting in which discussion takes place on neutral ground is something of an equivalent. But, more indirectly still, we need dramatists and script-writers who can allow their Christian faith to jut into human situations with self-authenticating competence.

A headmaster preparing to conduct a school assembly has to take account of the fact that he must prepare for the benefit of children and young people who are at best half-way to readiness for full Christian worship. He has to acknowledge that he can expect little more than goodwill and has to earn that. In many cases those participating come from homes that are disenchanted with accepted forms of religion. Prayer is a habit that is foreign. Over the years an appreciation of the value of silence and reflection on deep words can be expected, but in such a position a headmaster has to go gently and slowly if he wishes others to enter into and share the things which he values most. The evangelist at work today must learn this lesson.

A dogmatic declaration of the Gospel Billy-Graham-style makes little impression on the mobile technocrats who prize compassion but find little relevance in a Church when the Church seems stuck in a siding, maintaining a round of repetitive worship. "If you were God, would you want people to be worshipping you in this way?" they ask. "Is the Church really interested in truth?" is another of their questions. It is difficult to disarm those who sincerely believe that the Church has allowed itself to become preoccupied with its own survival and its own power. Such people are contemptuous of calculated attempts to be with-it in worship and are, very sensibly, waiting for the Church to show some signs of management-response to its all too apparent problems.

It is no good preaching the Gospel as though the Church and its misguided priorities did not exist. The Gospel cannot effectively be preached in a vacuum. If the Church is showing Christianity to be one thing (inward-looking, power-hungry, politically accommodating) all the preaching in the world will not convince the open-minded man that Christianity is really something quite different. He will not be brain-washed into disbelieving the evidence of his own eyes. After all, the price a man has to pay for becoming a Christian is church membership; he has to identify himself with one of these bodies which, in his view, are so abundantly unsatisfactory.

To deal with a situation of this kind the Church has

first to come down from its pedestal. It must put itself right before it ventures on the always delicate task of putting other people right. Until it does this it will gain no more than a severely qualified response from non-club-members.

In the interests of evangelism the Church must be prepared to put at risk its present security. It must be prepared to forfeit the support forthcoming from its adherents for the sake of adaptation to the role it should be playing today. The conventional religious club set-up must be measured against the secular, compassionate, inquiring men and women around us, and what is no more than traditional must be discarded if necessary.

Many people have said all this, but Evangelicals have (or should have) a particular reason for demanding reform: without such reform evangelism is impossible. Men will not take us seriously. They will not take us seriously so long as we pretend that the territorial distribution of clergymen on a medieval pattern is a suitable strategy for mission in a complex, mobile society. They will not take us seriously while we perpetuate an elaborate structure designed for a bygone age. They will not take us seriously while the Church is more interested in self-preservation than in mission. What it amounts to is this: we have the choice between backing the privileges inherent in the present set-up and going out looking for the lost sheep.

If reform is not forthcoming, then for the sake of our contemporaries we must think beyond our present limitations. "It's better that men should be disorderly saved than orderly damned: and that the Church be disorderly preserved than orderly destroyed," said Richard Baxter.

It may be true that Evangelicals sometimes over-estimate the importance of conversion and give it a primacy which others properly criticise as inordinate. After all, "getting conversions" is a poor aim in re-ligion, and is not given any great importance by Christ himself. Each of us has to learn to know and love God, and that means a never-ending quest for perfection; to this conversion as generally understood is a mere pre-liminary. At its best, however, Evangelicalism takes account of this and gets its priorities right. Worship is God-centred and not an oblique means of making other people into Christians. Like other Christians Evangeli-cals lose themselves in the wonder and glory of God— and, having found this for themselves, are more ready to share the wonder and delight that they are finding in Christ.

An open mind and a readiness to admit that you are wrong are endearing characteristics, and all the more endearing when found unexpectedly in authoritarian and supposedly inflexible people. It ought to be noted that these characteristics are now being displayed more readily by Evangelicals than was once the case, and that there are Evangelicals who are genuinely seeking answers wherever the answers may be found and how-ever surprising they may be.

CHAPTER THIRTEEN

Why are they disliked?

When the first heart transplant operations took place, a great deal of responsible argument took place on the ethics of the matter—the question of confirming the "donor" 's death, for example, and the question of divulging the names of those involved. At that time it was not uncommon to come across parish magazines in which issues such as these were ignored by vicars who used this new step in surgery as a peg on which to hang a potted sermon on the new heart promised by the prophet Ezekiel. The prophet's metaphor is one which it is well to discuss when conversion is being considered, but it is little more than evasion to expatiate on it when the subject on the agenda is transplant surgery.

The "new heart" issue illustrates one way in which Evangelicals allow themselves to be betrayed into a kind of tub-thumping which is immensely unattractive to intelligent people. Christianity is reduced to a few simple slogans which are waved in front of outsiders at every opportunity. If only people would turn to Christ, it is asserted or implied (mostly asserted), our problems would be over. So means are found by which outsiders can be brought to a place (usually a church pew) where one slogan or another can be brandished before them. If only they would take note of these slogans, it is suggested, life would be altogether different.

The outsider who has problems of his own to consider (what is the most tactful way to encourage his teenage son to choose his girl-friends more sensibly? Should he pay more than he can reasonably afford for a private school education for his son? Can he stretch a point about that new model he is to sell—after all, his livelihood depends upon it?) finds that the slogans do not do justice to his situation. He concludes that he can expect little help from those who have thought less deeply about the human predicament than he himself has, so he leaves the slogan-shouters alone in future— and who can blame him?

Smug, small-minded, blinkered, superficial, insensitive, authoritarian, bigoted and illiterate: all these pejoratives have at some time or another been levelled at Evangelicals—and not without reason.

A man who has cut Christianity down to something he can manage and then condemns others for not accepting his interpretation can reasonably be described as small-minded. It is not unknown for Evangelicals to demonstrate this outlook. To ignore what perceptive writers are contributing to the intellectual life of one's own generation because they happen to notice things which are distasteful to Evangelicals is to be small-minded. Yet how many sermons preached in Evangelical churches show a lack of awareness of the searching criticism of life which is offered by contemporaries who, although they may not be Christians, have eyes open to things which Christians very often miss altogether? It must be remembered that until William Wilberforce, Thomas Clarkson and the rest agitated about the scandal of slavery, most Christians accepted it unhesitatingly as a divinely ordered plan. In the case of slavery it was Christians (including Evangelical Christians) who sounded the alarm, but it has not been Evangelical Christians who have been foremost in campaigning for civil rights for the oppressed. Nor is it Evangelicals who have been first to identify themselves with the under-privileged, although this is a strong note in the Gospels. If other Christians are marching in support of equal rights for the under-privileged, it is unbecoming for Evangelicals to assert that the powers that be are ordained of God and to allow gross discrimination and injustice to continue. Sometimes it seems that Evangelicals are too busy attempting to get conversions to notice the living standards of their neighbours. A preoccupation with "souls" leaves little energy to understand how slums and poverty degrade human beings.

As far as some Evangelicals are concerned, problems like racial discrimination do not exist. They are blinkered people. Perhaps their circumstances are favourable and they are ignorant of the pressures experienced by other men. It may be that they live a life

H

of unvarying routine, meeting the same small circle every day, meeting their Christian friends at the weekend, living the repetitive suburban life that so many people live today. They do not dip into the rich, startling, mind-stretching, eye-opening fund of literature freely available in their local library; instead, they solemnly read the latest "sound" book and imbibe the latest "sound" opinion. If people choose to live a blinkered life along these lines, they are, of course, perfectly free to do so; they are making a choice which is made by millions of people, Christians and otherwise. But if an unadventurous choice is made, it is rash to presume to lecture the adventurous ones on matters beyond the experience of the cloistered stay-at-homes. People in blinkers should confine themselves to guiding other people in blinkers. Let the blind lead the blind, in fact, while the sighted ones are out exploring.

Evangelicals sometimes are superficial. Like other clergymen, Evangelical clergymen in big demanding parishes have little time for wide reading. Like other clergymen, they are expected to preach too much, and they are reduced to shuffling the same thoughts into a different order rather than finding time to wrestle with new areas of human experience and to deepen their understanding of the mysterious issues of life and death. A stream cannot rise higher than its source, and lay people are not generally more spiritual than their vicars. Stock answers tend to prevail.

Glib answers are not well received today; nor is authoritarian advice on every department of life. But all too easily those who have found that Christ gives meaning in the midst of the human predicament give the impression of having found ready-made answers too, answers to such diverse problems as the upbringing of children, censorship, acceptable standards in entertainment and the place of private enterprise. Those who have given thought to these problems and wrestled with the disciplines involved do not, naturally, take kindly to slick answers imposed from outside.

Insistence on the need for conversion is often coupled with a failure to understand other aspects of the human predicament. It is all very well to say that the Scripture hath concluded all under sin, but the enthusiastic Christian who dismisses all modern drama as an expression of materialistic humanism or as one of the devil's sidelines will not get a friendly reception from the person who takes drama seriously—and nor will he deserve to.

Evangelicals sometimes forget that if you are setting out to gain the confidence of another person, one who happens to show sensitivity and judgment, you should think twice before you start if you happen to be philistine, unimaginative and uncreative. A blundering religious propagandist can easily do his cause more harm than good in such circumstances. In any case such a person plainly owes it to himself to give attention to a neglected (and therefore scruffy) department of his life;

he would do well to take lessons from the person whose eyes he is proposing to open.

A man who never reads Shakespeare and thinks Shakespeare has nothing to offer to the Christian is a man who should think very carefully before he goes around recommending other people to read the Bible every day. He is in danger of showing himself to be the impoverished person he is. Indeed, it would probably do him more good than harm if he left his Bible reading for a few days and caught up on his Shakespeare. To neglect all else for the sake of religious exercises suggests a glint in the eye that is sufficient to warn off any man of goodwill. Holiness by subtraction is not a formula that appeals to anybody outside Evangelical circles—and there is no reason why it should; it is not the formula found in the Bible.

A cavalier attitude to something you do not understand is a sure way of prejudicing your cause, whatever it may be. The non-Evangelical may well feel he is party to a case of pearls before swine in reverse; he (the non-Evangelical) has a pearl, and he is wasting it by putting it before a boorish person who has been so preoccupied with religion that he has not had time to develop his critical faculties. Who can blame such a person for avoiding his boorish acquaintance next time?

The Evangelical may be a bore rather than a boor. He never discovers this because his acquaintances are too gentle to make this plain to him; they merely bury themselves in their newspapers when they see him enter the train. They know his routine backwards and they know that nothing new can be expected. It is surely something of an achievement to turn the spontaneity and sparkle of Jesus Christ into a stodgy, ponderous line of propaganda, but it has been managed, and it has been managed by Evangelicals, amongst others.

Our contemporaries know that Jesus was no mere phrase-monger. J. B. Phillips has made that plain. Jesus did not deliver set-piece orations to crowds of people, whether they were listening or not. He was not a bore. He confounded expectations and went off, as it seemed, at a tangent, only to make a point with such devastating effectiveness that his questioner was temporarily demolished and had to creep away to reconstruct his view of life. If Jesus had been predictable and magisterial it is doubtful whether he would have retained the affection and (doubtless often stupefied) loyalty of busy fishermen who were always free to go back to their nets. Like the *Daily Mirror*, Jesus made a habit of starting where men were and looking honestly at the problems that puzzled them. It is true that he also made a habit of introducing them to problems that ought to have been puzzling them and were not, but when he did this it is plain that he did it in such a way as to carry them with him; he questioned, gave concrete examples and provoked them endlessly into thinking harder than they had ever thought in their lives.

Nobody could have called him predictable; it is extremely unlikely that men thought of him as garrulous and repetitious.

Is it surprising that our contemporaries are disappointed when they look inside our churches? And Evangelicals can scarcely claim that in this respect they are streets ahead of other Christians. For one thing Evangelicals are subject to temptations exceeding those of other men; where other clergymen find it necessary to preach sermons, Evangelical preachers must preach *long* sermons; where other Christians can find time for *joie de vivre*, Evangelicals must theologise about their pleasures. After the good-humoured spontaneity of the Christ of the Gospels the Christ preached by Evangelicals often suffers by comparison.

A not inconsiderable factor in accounting for the poor esteem enjoyed by Evangelicals is a simple failure in public relations. People simply do not realise that Evangelicals exist. They never meet Evangelicals (because Evangelicals are too heavily engaged in church meetings with other Evangelicals) and their only recollection of anything at all in that field is an ill-printed tract or a bellicose clergyman who refused to baptise their baby boy. Evangelical societies are poor at public relations; the publicists that there are in the Church at large are not Evangelicals; so the Evangelical case goes by default.

Together with others Evangelicals have incurred their share of odium as being obscurantist and authoritarian in an age which if it values anything at all values free inquiry. Mobile technocrats do not take kindly to an institution which is seen to be occupying static positions and to be unready to respond to a living situation. With what has every appearance of being an unconvincing, diffident, simple-minded faith in the Bible as the Word of God, Evangelicals seem to be at least as static and unresponsive as any other section of the Church.

It is nothing new for long-winded and flat-footed religious propagandists to receive something less than esteem. In Ben Jonson's day the odious Tribulation and Ananias and their friends found it necessary to cast

> Before your hungry hearers, scrupulous bones,
> As whether a Christian may hawk or hunt;

Now, of course, the hungry hearers will be obliged to deliberate on whether they should drink or dance. Particulars change, but the general cast of thought is unchanging, and it is a cast of thought which is singularly unattractive to the school of Ben then or now.

CHAPTER FOURTEEN

Did Keele change anything?

"Keele '67" was an event that made young Evangelicals jubilant. It also surprised outsiders. For the National Evangelical Anglican Congress meeting on the wet and windy campus of Keele University alongside the M 6 in April, 1967, showed Evangelicals (about 1,000 of them, with a preponderance of clergymen; it was a mid-week conference) buckling down to specific problems, instead of indulging in doctrinal day-dreaming or tub-thumping. In the groups and final sessions delegates had to declare where they stood and to make policy choices.

The outstanding effect of Keele was to deal a death-blow to the idea of an Evangelical unity existing as a kind of alternative to the ecumenical movement. This particular will-o'-the wisp was extinguished once and for all—to the accompaniment of protestations of ever-lasting friendship to Evangelicals in other Churches than the Church of England. (The protestations were received with coolness by Free Church Evangelicals.)

Keele '67 in fact set Church of England Evangelicals squarely in the historic Church. Loyalty to the historic

Church (which, for the present, is the Church of England) came before loyalty to Evangelicals wherever they might be found. This settled the outstanding question in any discussions on church unity: what is the Church? Keele decided that it was a historic, continuing body, from which it was wrong to sever oneself unless it had become so apostate as to be intolerable.

The immensity of this decision must not be ignored. At the back of many Evangelical minds is a hazy picture of an uncorrupted Church which is seen as the ancestor and example of Evangelicals today. Such a Church, it is dreamily thought, must have been Evangelical because we who inherit its best characteristics are ourselves Evangelical. As a comforting illusion this is doubtless satisfactory; as fact or theory it is derisory and misleading. Nobody in his right mind could call the New Testament Church either perfect or Evangelical. It was full of quarrelsome partisans, half-baked preachers and an appreciation of the necessity for compromise. Its outstanding leader was authoritarian and stood no nonsense. It was a body that cherished poetry and tolerated incest. It was in fact as mixed and muddled as any Church today.

Even where the essentially mixed nature of the New Testament Church has been recognised by Evangelicals, there has been a ruling principle of "come out from among them, and be ye separate". The whole Church with its range of opinions has been too great a practical problem for the earnest Evangelical; to get anything done it has seemed necessary to choose a platform and unite Christians on that basis. Evangelicals have done what others have done, but the platform has come to serve almost instead of the Church; even the label "Christian" has been restricted to equal "Evangelical".

Keele knocked the stuffing out of this misconception. It accepted the Church as a body of baptised people, containing Evangelicals and others. It decided that church unity must be sought within the historic Church rather than among Evangelicals in various Churches. By doing this it bitterly disappointed non-Anglican Evangelicals and uprooted what had for a generation been a corner-stone of Evangelical membership of the Church of England—the view that the Church of England is a federation of parish churches which allows its members to lead an independent life and pay a minimum subscription.

The illusion of a form of church unity restricted to Evangelicals from all the Churches was shattered at Keele, and with it was shattered an aspiration after monolithic Evangelical unity within the Church of England; for the other significant development at Keele was the emergence of independent opinion and argument. Such had not been the original intention of the organisers of N E A C, it seems, but in the event specific application to some of the controversial issues of the day showed itself. Suddenly, Evangelicalism came alive. From being a dull, inert, old-fashioned conformity to a received pattern it turned into a questioning, self-critical search for sensible answers to questions before Christians today. Submission to patriarchal authority melted as young Evangelicals looked at the received answers (or evasions) and found them wanting. It was as though Evangelicalism had come out of the tunnel and men had begun to breathe again.

Of course, Evangelicalism was still years behind other Christians, as the conference statement revealed. N E A C discovered that we were living in a secular society, that we needed a new prayer book, that Christian education was of first importance, and it ingenuously set down its views as it blinked in the new-found light.

Deferential nods were made where precision was required. Sunday observance, women's ministry, mission areas and the opportunities provided by the mass media were acknowledged and made the subject of platitude. The length of the statement and the timing of the conference (it ended on a Friday) meant that despite brilliant administrative work with stencils, etc., the conference was hardly noticed by the dailies (cf. the space gained each year by the Modern Churchmen's conference). On the way home from Keele some delegates were already having qualms about the statement they had approved. But it would have been wrong to expect too much after years of neglect.

Did Keele make any difference? Was it a decisive conference that set Evangelicals on a new course, or did the Evangelicals merely turn over in their sleep?

Undoubtedly Keele *said* a great many progressive things
—about a principal weekly service of Communion, for
example—but, as with the Lambeth Conference, local
willingness to implement points made at Keele varies
immensely. It is probably true to say that Keele served
to confirm Evangelicals in their existing preferences.
The radicals were encouraged to develop their radical
views; the reactionaries became more than ever convinced that matters had got out of hand and that the
old ways must be vigorously defended.

The forces of reaction are strong. This has been
demonstrated by the failure of N E A C to set in
motion a continuing reconsideration among Evangelicals. Despite well attended follow-up meetings and the
continued existence of the N E A C organising committee (now in a state of suspended animation),
"Forward from Keele" remains an empty aspiration.
Evangelicalism has a built-in bias towards conservatism,
and this not only in theology. The bias is evident in the
focal points of Evangelical power—the societies; these
are for the most part of long standing, which is another
way of saying that they are in the hands of old men.
Evangelical societies and organisations vie with one
another ostensibly to foster the Evangelical interest.
The Church of England Evangelical Council regards
itself as having an authority unique among all these
organisations, but this view is not widely shared. The
C E E C is a self-appointing body and cannot claim to
be representative. The Federation of Diocesan

Evangelical Unions regards *itself* as having a position of leadership, owing to its representative nature; but the F D E U rarely meets and is almost unknown to most Evangelicals. The component members of F D E U, the Diocesan Evangelical Unions, are slowly overhauling themselves and beginning to admit lay members, but they are frequently stodgy and clergy-dominated. Amongst other organisations there is the Fellowship of Evangelical Churchmen, which regards itself as representative of the Evangelical interest throughout the country (but is not so regarded by those outside its membership), Church Society (which rarely makes any impact outside its limited membership) and the Church Pastoral-Aid Society (which disclaims any interest in ecclesiastical politics but makes determined efforts to preserve the present parochial system and private patronage). Various shadowy bodies such as the Keele organising committee continue to have a finger in the pie because Evangelical committees once formed find it hard to extinguish themselves.

With such a wealth of societies and committees—not to mention private ones such as the Eclectics (for clergymen only, more or less)—the possibility of anything actually being done is remote. The Evangelical structure is the Church of England in miniature: an arrangement designed to resist change (or so it appears in practice). The Keele delegates may have talked their heads off; they may have produced a statement which is, in parts, at least tentatively inclined to revolution.

But the good intentions are smothered in the committees which (however unrepresentative they may be) are the true centres of power in the Evangelical world.

If the redundant (and almost inevitably obstructive) organisations could be axed, if a genuinely representative structure could be set up to establish a connection between the decision-takers and grass-roots Evangelicals—perhaps via D E U s and C E E C—there might be some chance of decisions taken at Keele having some effect. As it is the good intentions generated at Keele are stultified. But with all this, there must be yet another proviso. Evangelicals must learn to trust one another. Basically it is not inept organisation or multiplied committees which stifle Evangelical initiative; it is the fact (of which the multiplied organisations are symptomatic) that one Evangelical, or one group of Evangelicals, distrusts another. Each is convinced that he, or his small group, is right, whatever other Evangelicals may say. Co-operation cannot be built where there is a lack of trust.

It may possibly be true that the continued existence of Evangelicals within the Church of England turns on the retention of private patronage. It may be true that a weekly service of the Lord's Supper as the principal Sunday service is a desirable pattern. It may be true that the *Series Two* Communion service does not demonstrate as unmistakably as the 1662 form the doctrine of justification by faith alone. All these things

may or may not be true. But on these points Evangelicals are simply not agreed. It is idle to pretend that
they are. And to these points could be added a multitude of others. The fact must be faced that Evangelicals
are not in a position to gain particular ends within the
Church of England. They are not a united body. They
have no agreed aims and policy which they are prepared to forward. While they are in disagreement on a
variety of issues they must remain weak. To think
otherwise (and some Evangelicals do hopefully think
otherwise) is to live in cloud-cuckoo-land. Omelettes
cannot be made without eggs being broken; and it is
doubtful whether the Evangelical interest can be advanced without some Evangelicals being offended and
some organisations being sent packing. The time must
come when Evangelicals face these issues and decide
where they stand. The result will be a parting of the
ways. At present the painful moment is being post-
poned. Evangelicals stay together by going in all direc-
tions at once and pretending that distance does not
really separate friends. Evangelical unity is strictly
doctrinal and theoretical; it crumbles when it has to
make a practical choice. It has yet to be seen whether
Keele will result in Evangelicals being prepared to co-
operate—and being prepared to pay the price that
co-operation involves.

CHAPTER FIFTEEN

Death and renewal

If the foregoing account is accepted, the first people in need of renewal are Evangelicals. Blind spots, sacred cows and a refusal to face facts impose crippling limitations. But a prior question must be faced: can Evangelicals, who believe so much, who believe it uncompromisingly and enthusiastically, survive at all in an age when men believe little and give assent rather than enthusiastic support to the Christian religion?

Evangelical belief is clearly articulated, propositional and therefore vulnerable. It is impossible for an Evangelical to slip from one doctrinal position to another, eluding his opponents, only to emerge triumphantly at the end claiming to have preserved his faith and his integrity even if nobody else accepts the claim. Evangelicals long ago acquired the habit of sticking to their doctrinal guns despite the opposition. Given the tight network and the mutual support system functioning as efficiently as ever, it is unlikely that Evangelicalism will suffer from mass defections by doctrinal malcontents.

There is no call for Evangelicalism to abandon its

distinctive doctrines, to tone down its submission to the sovereign authority of Scripture, the atoning death of Christ and the justification of man by grace through faith. There may be scope for these doctrines to be presented with more sensitivity and imagination; there may be scope too for a commonsense recognition of the poetic content of much biblical literature that is all too frequently interpreted prosaically. But at its best Evangelicalism takes the Bible seriously and brings to it a serious and inquiring frame of mind; it would be immeasurably sad if this submissive attitude to biblical revelation were lost.

What is at issue, then, is not the survival of Evangelicalism as a biblical version of Christianity; having survived thus far, Evangelicalism is unlikely to be shipwrecked by theologians who stand Christianity on its head. What is at issue is whether Evangelicalism will survive if it does what the argument of this book indicates is necessary: die in order to be reborn. At the present moment Evangelicalism is not sick or dying; but it *is* wedded to obsolete and damaging habits and assumptions. If it sticks to those habits it will survive in the form in which we know it now; if it renounces its habits, Evangelicalism as we know it will be dead, like the lion in Samson's riddle, and something new (honey? vinegar?) will appear. What that something new will be, nobody can tell.

Evangelicalism as we know it is in fact an inadequate expression of biblical Christianity. Its blind spots and sacred cows, its dubious traditions and prejudices, its failure to be both biblical and realistic, its partiality for those aspects of the Christian revelation which it finds congenial and its shunning of those aspects which it finds inconvenient make it an unsatisfactory form of Christian faith. It may be better than most other forms of the Christian faith in the eyes of those who measure their Christianity against the New Testament revelation, but it is still defective.

To repeat, this is *not* to say that Evangelicalism has distorted or denied basic Christian doctrine; it has indeed preserved orthodox Christian belief at a time when many inside the Church have so twisted Christian doctrines that it is difficult to see how they can be called Christians. But, preoccupied with its task of preserving the truth, Evangelicalism has become conditioned by the harsh necessities of survival; it is in danger of losing its own soul by virtue of being over-determined to ensure its continued existence, to keep its stake in the organised Church. It is suffering from a hardening of the arteries at a time when Christians should be more flexible and adaptable than ever before. Like the rest of the Church, Evangelicals are stiff and stodgy, intimidated by precedent and tradition.

The first need of the Church today is not Anglican-Methodist unity or synodical government or a revision of the parochial system; the first need of the Church is renewal. Undoubtedly renewal will express itself in some way in the fields of church unity, lay responsibility and the deployment of the clergy, but renewal must come first. A Church that is neat and tidy but dead will not prove sufficient for the 1970s, although it is possible to imagine an untidy, disorganised Church capturing men's allegiance in the 1970s despite its defects. It is as leaders on the road to renewal that Evangelicals now have a high duty to perform.

Shortcomings galore and follies innumerable there may be amongst them, but Evangelicals have the merit of keeping their eyes on the goal. Evangelicals are Christians who believe that Christianity is Christ, and that to become a Christian is to meet Christ. They also believe (when they are true to their own best convictions) that the Church is a pilgrim Church, a Church on the move, a Church moving on into unknown territory. At all times such an emphasis is healthy; at a time like the present, when the Church is bogged down in unity and reorganisation schemes, such an emphasis is vital. Only too frequently do the Churches give the impression of being concerned above all to preserve their own existence; if at such a time a group of Christians are urgently recalling their fellow-believers to their pilgrim task, that group can perform a service out of all proportion to its size.

The first thing that Evangelicals must do then is to be true to their principles. They must submit themselves to the Word of God and actively seek the truth rather than think they possess it already. They must not love Evangelicalism or Evangelical traditions more than biblical truth itself. They must be prepared to acknowledge that they themselves are the first people to need the reforming that comes from the Word of God. They must be prepared for something new, something that has not been seen before, some new expression of Christianity that will not be Evangelicalism, or Puritanism, or Reformed Christianity but some new manifestation altogether.

It is no exaggeration to say that what is needed now is the death of Evangelicalism as we know it, a death to that version of Christianity which claims to confide in the power of God but in fact trusts in princes and entrenched positions. If Evangelicalism is to command respect it must survive by force of example and weight of argument, not by dint of patronage, the divine right of clergymen and stubborn resistance to innovation. The new shape of Evangelicalism must include what the present body does not include—a readiness to mix on equal terms with intelligent, sceptical agnostics (who may in fact take a more serious view of religious issues than many who habitually recite the Creed Sunday by Sunday) and with non-Evangelical Christians (who may in fact take a more serious view of such basic issues as the place of women in the Church than many who claim to be guided by the New Testament but are manifestly given to prejudice).

The death of Evangelicalism means a death to a form of religion that is too spiritual to take account of practical necessities. It is not true religion to shut your eyes to the need for regular procedure in the business of the Church. It is not true religion to suppress other points of view, to manipulate unwitting voters, to evade issues brought to the fore by lay people in the proper processes of Church government. Yet in pursuit of a spiritual goal Evangelicals, like others, have done these things in their parochial church councils.

The death of Evangelicalism means an end to the deferential habit of mind that looks to leaders for ready-made solutions. The Gospel does not spell the end of human initiative or creative effort (or, for that matter, of controversy). Nor does the Gospel result in pallid puppets jerking their way through an ecclesiastical ballet.

The death of Evangelicalism means an end to the monarchical ministry which stultifies lay responsibility, depriving ordinary Christians of an effective voice in the selection of their minister and denying them the opportunity to take risks in the service of Christ. The death of Evangelicalism means an end to the uniformly full-time parochial ministry owing more to the feudal system than to the New Testament. The death of Evangelicalism means an end to the one-man band.

If Evangelicalism is to arise from the dead, it must arise as a body which is ready to consider cultural questions on their merit, not to bring to cultural issues pre-conceived judgments doubtfully derived from Scripture. If Evangelicalism is to deserve a place in the 1970s it must be turned inside-out. It must relegate the routine affairs of the religious club to the bottom of the agenda and show itself determined to get into the dust and heat of the arena. Instead of waiting for the sense of advancing years and approaching death to bring a steady flow of recruits into the Church, it must concentrate its major effort on confronting young middle-aged people with a meaningful interpretation of the Gospel.

Evangelicalism will not survive if it is not renewed; neither, of course will the Church. It is not enough for Evangelicals to say the equivalent of "We have Abraham to our father". An impeccable doctrinal pedigree and a set of worn-out taboos are not going to be sufficient equipment for the voyage through the 1970s. Without renewal—and that means a creative, inquiring, risk-taking attitude to problems and opportunities—Evangelicalism is doomed to be a historical curiosity.

Renewal means a readiness to follow the intrinsic logic of Evangelicalism and to express it in practice. It means more innovations such as the introduction of lay elders in an Evangelical parish in Bristol. It means a more positive approach to women's ministry. It means a greater readiness to renounce the cosiness and security of the existing parochial system and to open up new forms of ministry where those forms are needed. Renewal means listening to the young as well as the old. Renewal means being the first candidate in the queue for renewal.

Renewal will not come painlessly to Evangelicals.

There are too many privileges and customs attached to
the present order of things for a break to be made easily
and cleanly. Clergymen who have known a lifetime of
running their parishes for the benefit of docile and submissive parishioners will not easily adopt a new role as
religious teachers and advisers providing specialised in-
struction and ministry while lay people play their
appropriate part in managing the affairs of the
Christian community. Nor will renewal come easily to
those Evangelical laymen who have been content to see
their vicar play a paternalist role while they happily fail
to assume their responsibilities.

CHAPTER SIXTEEN

Advance party

Evangelicals are not in possession of the whole truth about everything. They are weak in their understanding of the secular society, sleepy about issues involving social justice, unaware of the formative powers of institutions (and of the place of the Church in particular) and almost totally ignorant about getting their message across effectively in a technological society. Evangelicals have little that is helpful to say about the training of ministers of the Gospel, few experiments in hand in the way of group ministries and only a groping awareness of the relationship between Evangelical Christians and the non-Evangelical majority.

Crippling as these limitations are, it remains true that Evangelicals have a unique responsibility. However ill equipped they are to discharge that responsibility, it is their privilege to act as an advance party of the Church, pointing out the direction the Church should take and exploring the ground for the rest to follow. To be an Evangelical is not (though it has come to seem so) to perform a static role; it is to push ahead into unknown country in the service of the Gospel; it is to lead

the pilgrim Church through virgin country. Evangelicalism as we now know it is not able to do this; a renewed Evangelicalism should be able not only to do the
task but delight in it.

A Church that is in constant danger of following
after will-o'-the-wisps such as stewardship and
elaborate Lent discussion courses needs a reconnais-
sance party. A Church needs in fact what the children
of Israel needed in the wilderness—a group of intrepid
scouts led by men like Joshua and Caleb to push ahead
and see how big the grapes and the giants are. This
function Evangelicals at their best have succeeded in
performing. They have asserted the primacy of the
Gospel and the authority of the Word of God when the
Church as a whole has been tempted to ignore its
marching orders.

Evangelicals have the responsibility of standing for
the truth as they see it; they also have the responsibility
of prodding the Church into resuming its pilgrimage.
As has been said so many times by so many people, the
Church has allowed itself to be manœuvred into a
siding while the main traffic rushes past—with the
result that Christians have to make a choice between
serving in the context of an irrelevant Church and
serving outside the Church among the people who need
Christ. With their sense of priorities Evangelicals are
superbly placed to make the best of this situation—calling the Church on the one hand to remember its mobile
role and reminding secular men on the other that the

Gospel is primarily a relationship with Christ rather than membership of a Church.

In effect Evangelicals have a new role before them, that of disturbers of the *status quo*. This is the opposite of their customary one, but it is one that their theological position now requires. It is they who should now, in the interest of the Gospel, be challenging the widespread notion that every parish should have an organ, a hall and a magazine. These cherished components of the Anglican scene are, in days when the Church should be in trekking trim, luxuries which cannot be afforded. At least, they are luxuries in many localities. To invest in an organ is like investing in a Rolls-Royce; no man does it unless he knows he can afford the regular outgoings. Many parishes confess their inability to afford an organ by their frantic organ appeals and their failure to pay their organists an appropriate salary scale.

It is the simplest thing in the world to say that we should cut our cloth according to our means, that we should curb the grandiose ideas that we have inherited from our past; it is Evangelicals who should be saying it. It is the simplest thing in the world to say that we should not design and pay for new buildings as one-day-a-week buildings—and then scrape together the money to build a hall alongside; again, it is Evangelicals who should be saying this. It is the simplest thing in the world to look objectively at the effectiveness of parish magazines and ask whether the money and time are well spent. It is Evangelicals who should be taking the objective look.

Organs, halls and magazines are symptomatic. What really needs to be considered is the whole range of issues involved in the inherited set-up of the Church of England. Designed to minister efficiently to static, half-literate Christian Englishmen, the complicated set-up is hollow and deserted. Men no longer look to the Church to arrange their lives for them; but the Church continues to operate an elaborate set-up as though they do. An excellent World Council of Churches publication *The Church for Others* containing two reports on the missionary structure of the congregation puts the issue squarely. The Church of England needs men who will compel it to face this issue of "morphological fundamentalism" and "heretical" structures. Why should those men not be Evangelicals?

If Christ is to be effectively Lord of the Church, each generation of Christians must ensure that His dominion is appropriately evident in the circumstances over which they have control. Each generation must do its own work; it cannot rely on the work—however good it may have been in its time—of a preceding generation. It is to this work that the present generation of Christians is having to apply itself painfully, and it is Evangelicals who must take a leading part in the operation.

In some respects the pioneering is already afoot. Young Evangelicals have produced *A Eucharist for the*

Seventies, and churches like St George's, Leeds, have taken advantage of the flexibility afforded by *Series Two* to experiment with so revolutionary a practice (for Anglicans) as that of passing the bread along the pews from person to person at Holy Communion. Evangelicals have led the way with coffee-bar campaigns (as in Woking, Surrey), and home meetings are probably as common in Evangelical parishes as anywhere. The London College of Divinity is gently breaking out of the strait-jacket confining the training of men for the ministry.

Evangelicals have done much in the field of church music, hymns and songs. *Youth Praise*, the song book for young people, has shown that creative minds are at work already. Free-lance Gospel singers like Jack and Pauline Filby and the group calling themselves Los Picaflores from South America have demonstrated that a musical ministry outside the normal parochial pattern is a possibility. Living church music is scarcely all it ought to be in the Church of England; having made a start, Evangelicals now have the opportunity of setting the pace.

Another matter for Evangelicals to explore is some better pattern than our monarchical form of ministry in which the vicar does everything and makes all the decisions and the dutiful lay people do what they are told and applaud. This is *not* the pattern found in the New Testament and it is not the type of ministry which is likely to prove most effective in our mixed, mobile,

bustling society. Whether we like it or not, specialisa-
tion is being forced upon the Church, and the result is
likely to be something much nearer the diversity of
ministries found in the New Testament than the
omnicompetent pastor and the grateful, addle-headed
sheep.

Evangelicals can show their openness to Scripture
and their eagerness to be on the march by reconsider-
ing the parson's freehold and patronage. The Gospel
and its ministers do not need to be defended by legal
and financial manœuvres of this kind; better a voluntary
or part-time ministry earning its money elsewhere and
consequently able to speak its mind freely than a ministry trammelled by an unearned income, ignorant of
the day-to-day burdens borne by ordinary mortals with
big mortgages and strong competitors, and obligated by
gifts from a complacent congregation.

One respect in which Evangelical pioneering is called
for is the matter of giving responsibility to young men.
At present the prevailing tone of the Church of England is patriarchal. If a man is not *actually* old, it is to
his advantage to *look* old. Seniority is of decisive importance. At any given time there are probably fewer
than half a dozen bishops under fifty amongst the English diocesans and their suffragans. An institution with
an elderly leadership does not readily change its ways.
It is not of course possible for Evangelicals to do much
about putting young men into positions of leadership in
the Church of England. We shall go on having elderly

bishops for a long time yet. But it *is* possible for Evangelicals to set an example in this matter, and this would be facilitated if rank-and-file Evangelicals would pay a little less deference to father-figures, and if Evangelical leaders gave more scope to young men. At the present time Evangelicals are very much inclined to wait to hear what the Rev —— —— or Dr —— has said before they declare their own opinions. A little more honest argument would enable genuine leadership to emerge—and that would mean the emergence of a number of leaders who would probably not agree on a good many issues.

Another respect in which Evangelicals should be explorers rather than foot-draggers is the ministry of women. The Christian Gospel plainly contained in embryo (as it contained so many things) the abolition of slavery. It also contained and contains the abolition of sex discrimination. But this is still contested in the Church. There are still those who deny women the right to exercise a ministry—rather like the Brethren who will not allow women to open their mouths in prayer in a mixed assembly. But the removal of sex-disqualification is widely regarded as implicit in Galatians 3: 28, and Evangelicals have been notable in the backing they have given to women's ministry—even though one women's college after another is shutting its doors for the last time because women are not persuaded that the Church is at present taking their ministry seriously. Women could bring to the ministry of the Church gifts complementary to those of men; an imbalance would be redressed; the Church would be seen to be true to its basic Gospel; the feverish situation in the women's organisations inside the Church would approach normality—these are great and desirable benefits. Evangelicals should determine that they will work to achieve them.

It is the fact that Evangelicals are (or claim to be) open to Scripture (and therefore open to new ideas and revolutionary impulses) that makes them an important group. Evangelicals, like other men, can shut their ears but they have shown in the past that they can hear what others cannot. It is this faculty which must be recovered. An advance party is not expected to know all the answers before it sets out; it goes off with its maps and keeps its eyes open. For this task Evangelicals, despite a certain lack of imagination, are peculiarly well suited.

At present, however, Evangelicals are as often as not hidebound, accepting as guidelines the traditions of men, loath to innovate, reluctant to exploit the potential that they undoubtedly have. When Evangelicals recover their nerve and venture ahead of the main body of Christians, they will amaze the Church. But he would be a daring man who would predict when such a recovery is likely to take place.

CHAPTER SEVENTEEN

Plotting a new course

Thirty years ago, any Evangelical who set out to speak about the future would automatically have been expected to deal with Daniel, Revelation, the capture of Jerusalem and the final rapture of the saints. Today his audience will expect him to deal with new patterns of worship, Church unity and parochial reform. The change is momentous, and it is resented by those who fear that in soft-pedalling its other-worldliness Evangelicalism is betraying its heritage. But for those Evangelicals who believe that the Christian faith must be both biblical and realistic the change of outlook is promising. Instead of indulging in a precipitate flight from urgent policy issues into doctrinal fantasy the present-day Evangelical is likely to be found sweating his way through a Church Assembly paper or a report from an Archbishops' Commission.

This generation of Evangelicals is living in days when the Church is timidly moving into unknown country. Compelled by circumstances to look out dusty maps and to examine the notes made by earlier pioneers, Evangelicals are discovering that the familiar tracks of 1662, royal supremacy and Calvinistic Articles had lulled them over the years into a familiar routine that had made them forget their fieldcraft. Keele '67 awoke the pilgrims to the new duties required of them in unfamiliar territory and rough weather. Aching limbs and dizzy heads bear witness to the painful experience this change of course is proving for the pilgrims, particularly the older ones among them.

What course must Evangelicals seek out and prescribe for the Church as it moves slowly and hesitantly into the 1970s? In which direction should the advance party lead? The answer will not be forthcoming without attention to the navigational problems involved, and it may well be the case that some pilgrims (Evangelical and otherwise) will be unable to follow the course once it is chosen. What follows is a number of brief references to the basic navigational factors involved in setting that course.

As the navigator takes his bearings and does his sums, he must now take as axiomatic the decision made at Keele to work within the historic Church. However painful it may be for Evangelicals outside the Church of England, the Evangelicals inside the Church of England are now committed to the hilt to a positive expression of reformed catholicism. Evangelicals now see themselves as members of the continuing historic Church. They are not Evangelicals who happen to be Anglicans. They are fully paid-up members of the

K

historic Church ready to think positively and con-
structively about their role.

What is required is an exploration of the significance
of reformed catholicism set against the sunset of the
Church of England and the Anglican Communion. A
new access of loyalty for the Church of England is not
enough. The Church of England is in the nature of
things a temporary expression of reformed catholicism;
the old pattern is in the melting-pot and a better pattern, we hope, is emerging. The fact that the old pattern
survived more or less unchanged for 300 years is a freak
of church history which will seem more and more in-
credible as we leave it further behind. What is going
forward now is a reshaping of the Church, which provides an opportunity of giving more precise, more
realistic expression to this principle of reformed
catholicism.

This is of prime importance. Evangelicals are not a
group of Christians owing nothing of any importance to
the historic Church. They are part of the historic
Church. For them the Church is not just a luxury
added to an already adequate faith. It is a continuing
body which is implicit in the Gospel and which must
be always under the judgment of Scripture. The
Church (including its Evangelical members) is always
in need of reform, and should always be on the move.
Evangelicals stand for reformed catholicism. They do
not stand for a non-Church type of Christianity; nor
do they dream of a perfect Church (composed entirely

of Evangelicals). At least, this is what Evangelicalism is essentially about; in practice it may not have been so clear. It is now the duty of Evangelicals to discover this and insist that it rules the policies of the Church.

In setting a new course the navigator must also give a proper place to radicalism. Of all men Evangelicals should be the most radical; the Evangelical emphasis, after all, is to go to the root of the matter, to go to the Bible for guiding principles and to be sceptical about any tradition or assumption that cannot survive close scrutiny by the light of God's Word. Deferential gestures were made at Keele in the direction of radicalism, but a more thoroughgoing radicalism must be incorporated into the plotting of a new course for the Church if it is to do anything more than take the pilgrims round in circles.

A radical understanding of the nature of the Church is called for. It must be clearly settled that the Church that Evangelicals want to see eventually is a Church (as biblical as possible in its formularies) including as many English Christians as possible (and eventually those Christians now known as Roman Catholics). For the present the resources of the existing Church of England must be applied where they are most needed—and this will inevitably mean an adjustment of the responsibilities of the Church Commissioners, a drive to demolish redundant buildings, and the declaration of mission areas in those places where the parochial system is plainly a farce.

A diversified ministry, male, female, full-time, part-time, voluntary, recognising the gifts God has given to Christian people, is another factor in this radical approach; so is the freedom of lay people to make responsible choices as leaders of the local Church (which includes freedom to make mistakes and some appropriate part to play in the appointment of full-time ministers). Local Christians should, indeed, be allowed the opportunity of ordering their own affairs within reasonable limits, and this should include the possibility of taking some definite steps to Church unity and introducing experimental services of worship.

To mention these things is to refer to matters that have been engaging the attention of radicals in the Church of England for years. But so far Evangelicals have not been noted for radical policies. Evangelicals have been more associated with policies that have been conservative to the point of timidity. If Evangelicalism is not radical, it will not survive; if it *is* radical, it may change out of all recognition. But there is really no choice, for the man who is determined to be ruled by Scripture is, willy-nilly, a radical. Perhaps we shall yet see Evangelicals evolving into biblical radicals who are calling the whole Church to a similar biblical radicalism.

Biblical radicalism is useless if it is not realistic. It is quite unrealistic, for example, to urge (as some have urged) that an appropriate aim for Evangelicals is to have an Evangelical in every pulpit in the Church of England. This is a view which implies the exclusion of anybody who is not an Evangelical; it is a denial of the fundamental toleration accorded by the Anglican Settlement to anyone whose views are compatible with the Articles and the Book of Common Prayer. Such a view is also question-begging, for it assumes that Evangelicals are of such a calibre as to be equal to such a responsibility; and this is manifestly untrue.

A new biblical radicalism will not be content with a plan of campaign that consists essentially in encouraging Evangelical recruits to enter the ministry in such numbers that they will in the end swamp the rest. Biblical radicalism will rely not on numbers but on ideas—and, of course, on spiritual quality. Biblical radicalism will attempt to shape a strategy, evangelistic and pastoral, for the whole Church.

Should biblical radicals, then, shape themselves into a party to replace the old Evangelical party of protest that is no more? Some would shudderingly spurn any such suggestion. The word "party" conveys to them the notion of distasteful political activity, of a regimented, squabblesome, small-minded clique intent on gaining its own dubious ends. But the word "party" can be used in another sense; it can signify a group agreed on aims and objectives and organised to achieve those aims by the political means appropriate to the body of which they are members.

In this sense, and in the context of a Church with clearly defined political machinery for decision-making, a biblical radical party is necessary. It will not be forthcoming for some considerable time yet. So far no policy commands sufficient agreement to unite Evangelicals; they are, politically speaking, in a state of disarray. If a renewed Evangelicalism is to make its mark, it must get itself organised and set itself to achieve its ends by honest political activity, by thrashing out aims, by collecting supporters, by winning votes, by campaigning for a place at the levers of power within the Church.

To those who find honest political activity distasteful it must be pointed out that the only other options available are (a) withdrawal from responsibility, and (b) dishonest political activity—i.e. intrigue, wire-pulling and covert manipulation. It is difficult to see a biblical radicalism which would be content with either of these options instead of honest political activity.

An incidental factor for the navigator to consider is a recognition of the necessity for compromise. It is scarcely necessary to point out that Evangelicals must be concerned with more than Evangelicalism; they must be concerned with the shape of the whole Church. This means meeting and working with Christians who are not Evangelicals and would never dream of becoming Evangelicals. It means compromise. The matter has been well put (in another context, it is true, but the same principle applies) by Professor A. J. P. Taylor: "This suggests indeed one of the strongest grounds for the popular objection to secret policy: the suspicion that every deal will be a dirty deal. And so in a sense it will. Agreement by diplomacy implies compromise; any compromise implies that you will get less than you want, probably indeed less than you think right. The alternative, however, is not to reach agreement, that is, to get nothing at all." (*Europe: Grandeur and Decline*, published by Penguin). We Christians can only live together in the Church if we are prepared to compromise. This was true of the Church at the time of the Council of Jerusalem; it was true when the Synod of Whitby was called to decide how Christians should have their hair cut; it is true today. To shut one's eyes to the necessity for compromise in any society that is to last more than five minutes is to live in cloud-cuckoo-land.

This is a difficult pill for Evangelicals to swallow. In the past Evangelicals have been fond of taking the view that they are the only legitimate Anglicans, that other types of Anglicanism are counterfeit, and that any departure from the Thirty-nine Articles (though not the services of the 1662 prayer book) is treachery. There is no avoiding the need to ask what the Church of England has always been about, what it is going to be about in the future, and what kind of Church is possible to sinners who, despite their new life in Christ, are still foolish and short-sighted men. We must ask, as we so often have to ask in life, what is *possible*. Evangelicals must be prepared to abandon some of their shibboleths and the need for this must be generally accepted.

In passing it may be said that respect for compromise

does not necessarily involve acceptance of a stratagem such as the proposed Services of Reconciliation. There is a difference between paradox which may be necessary to do justice to different aspects of the Christian revelation and a verbal ambiguity calculated to bear conflicting interpretations in the interests of a political solution to a Church unity problem.

At present the navigator has scarcely managed to get his maps on to the table. He is surrounded by vociferous companions who are pointing out that they will not co-operate if any one of half a dozen likely courses is chosen. Evangelicals are as vociferous and confused as anybody else. This is not a time for unity among Evangelicals; it is a time for argument, for purposeful consideration of possibilities. We must expect a lengthy period of clashing opinions before any measure of agreement is possible. He will best serve the interests of Evangelicals who compels Evangelicals to face issues, come to conclusions and make decisions. Not until this is done should Evangelicals imagine they are united. Not until then will Evangelicals command an influence proportionate to their numbers.

The choice before Evangelicals is plain. Either they look backward (fondly) at their cherished past and inward (sentimentally) at their delicate sensibilities — or they take the way of renewal. Renewal will mean seeking a new expression of reformed catholicism, and will mean being prepared to discover that it is different in many important respects from the traditional Evangelical interpretation of Church of England policies. Renewal will mean an exploration of biblical radicalism, a readiness to go to biblical roots and to shape organisation and strategy accordingly. Renewal will mean a readiness to be guided by principles rather than by expediency—and that may mean losing a stake in the *status quo* for the sake of some unknown good whose shape we cannot yet discern.

To set a course dictated by the foregoing considerations will result in plain speaking, wounded vanity and differences among Evangelicals. To set such a course will require Evangelicals to go out like Abraham into untracked territory. But how can this deter those who claim to be guided by Scripture and to be walking in the steps of those who, like Abraham, confided in God rather than in their comforting routine, and—again like Abraham—paid more attention to the unlikely commands of God than to the siren voices around them?

CHAPTER EIGHTEEN

Yet I am still an Evangelical

In this little book I have expressed a number of reserva-
tions about contemporary Evangelicalism. It may seem
that, holding the views I do, I should move hot-foot
out of the Evangelical camp. But this, I believe,
would be to do a disservice to my own convictions and
to my fellow-Evangelicals. It would be a disservice to
my own convictions because as I understand the
matter an Evangelical interpretation of the Gospel
rings true. It would be a disservice to my fellow-
Evangelicals because one of the most urgent needs in
the Evangelical camp is to accommodate men of varying
views.

I am content to be described as an Evangelical, if
others will allow me this title. As I have argued, I
believe that the Evangelical version of Christianity
ensures that certain vital aspects of Christianity are not
forgotten or overlaid. Those aspects include the inward-
ness of true religion, the impregnable standing of the
forgiven man in Christ, and the supreme authority of
Scripture. These are not the only vital aspects of

Christianity, but take these away and Christianity is seriously distorted. At least, this is my understanding of the matter. As well as finding that an Evangelical interpretation of the Christian faith rings true, I find that it is a generous interpretation. An Evangelical asks whether a man has faith in Christ, not whether he has been episcopally confirmed. An Evangelical asks (or should ask) what gifts God has given to a variety of people, not what man-made regulations limit the exercise of ministry. An Evangelical believes that Christianity is Christ, that God's mercies are covenanted in Christ, that man's proper response is to be identified in baptism with Christ's death and resurrection and to work out that identification during the remainder of his days.

Nothing would please me more than to be able to pack away my Evangelicalism, to agree with all Christian men and to be one tiny part of a truly international Church. I recognise that other Christians whose opinions are very different from my own have a great deal to teach me, and I recognise that they and I have far more in common than we sometimes think. (What we actually have in common tends to show itself when views on a piece of literature or a moral problem are being expressed.) But I find a difficulty. While there are differing views on the authority of Scripture and the securing of man's salvation, I am constrained to adopt what are known as Evangelical opinions. Soft-pedal the matter as I may, I find myself obliged to be not merely a Christian but an Evangelical Christian.

Certain things are basic to Evangelical Christianity, and it is the basic things that I admire. Other, less desirable, characteristics tend to become mixed into the basic stock and so we have in practice a blend of Evangelical doctrine, unexamined assumptions, concealed prejudices and plain error. At the present time it is a prime need to separate what is basic from what is merely traditional. I have sought to do some unblending in the present work.

Basically, then, I am happy to call myself, and to be called by others, an Evangelical. But I am not prepared to subscribe to certain features which come lock, stock and barrel in a package deal labelled "Evangelicalism". I am not convinced, for example, that enthusiasm for mass evangelism is a necessary concomitant of Evangelicalism. I believe, furthermore, that Evangelicals have allowed themselves to be betrayed into trivial views of such matters as the arts, politics and education. Where they have not been betrayed into accepting particular unsatisfactory views as a corollary of Evangelicalism, they have sometimes carried over a prevailing prejudice and imagined that by doing so they were being true to Scripture. I believe that Evangelicalism as we know it today is, like Old Testament Judaism, male-oriented. It also tends to be censorious (because it is suspicious of pleasure), punitive (because it confines its theological thinking overmuch to forensic categories), obscurantist (because it feels itself to be vulnerable on account of its clearly articulated theological position) and introverted (because it sees itself as an ill-regarded minority).

If I thought that being an Evangelical automatically involved accepting male domination, corporal punishment, bourgeois prejudices, trivial views, poor taste, a hankering after organising other people's lives, a refusal to look facts in the face, and a persecution complex, I should drop Evangelicalism like a hot brick. But I do not believe that these commonly occurring features are indispensable components of an Evangelical faith. Indeed, I think they are dangerous and objectionable and more than ripe for repudiation. An increasing number of Evangelicals are gradually doing the repudiating. When the process is well in hand, we shall see Evangelicalism in a fairer light. Christians with the same basic emphasis will differ widely in their habits, tastes and opinions. Evangelicals will no longer have the reputation of being morose and superficial kill-joys; instead they will display the variety and spontaneity that belong to the sons of God. Something of the exuberance one discovers in the account of the New Testament Church will come to the fore. It is this kind of Evangelicalism that I applaud, and it is this untrammelled Evangelicalism that appears in a rich diversity when Evangelicals are true to their deepest convictions.

I am thankful that there are numerous Evangelicals

who are devoted to Christ and his Gospel and who are at the same time amusing, witty, outrageous, properly sceptical, appreciative of drama and music and contemptuous of second-hand opinions. There remain seven thousand or more who have not bowed the knee to timidity, dullness and inert conformity. Many of them are among my closest friends. We need to hear more from such people. The most sincere and earnest man can be misinterpreted if by his silence he allows himself to be saddled with trivial and reactionary views that are thought to be of the essence of Evangelical Christianity. This is a time for men and women to dissociate themselves emphatically from the taboos and shibboleths which their convictions are widely held to require.

For myself, I am an Evangelical and trust I shall remain one. But I am neither a sabbatarian nor a teetotaller. I am not anti-theatre and I am not anti-leisure. I find myself interested in a great many matters which are not mentioned in the Bible and are hardly ever mentioned in Evangelical books. The fact that William Shakespeare and John Milton were not Evangelicals does not lessen my respect for their poetry. Where there is a job to be done in the world—whether it is bearing a political responsibility or coming to terms with administration in the midst of us fallen men—I believe the Christian should be foremost, looking the facts in the face, ready to get his hands dirty, not given to pussy-footing around the problem. To be an

Evangelical means to search out the heart of the Gospel and put first things first (but not to put them second and third as well); this is the kind of Evangelical I should like all Christians to be; this is the kind of Evangelical I wish to be myself.